I KNEW JESUS BEFORE HE WAS A CHRISTIAN

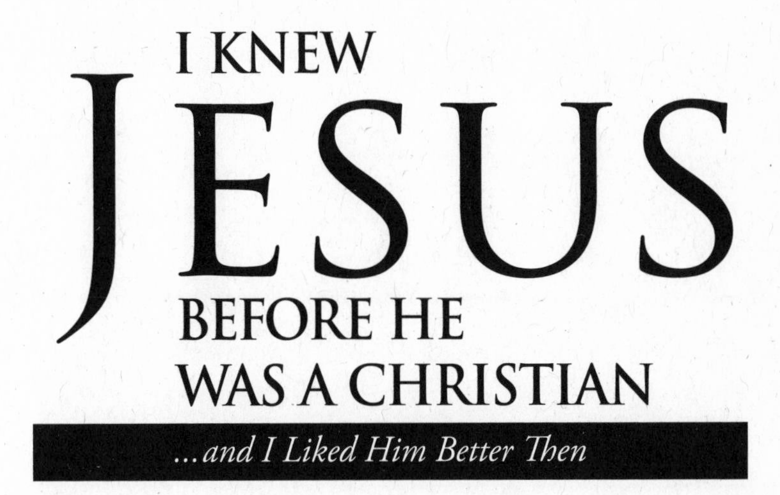

RUBEL SHELLY

I Knew Jesus before He Was a Christian

. . . and I Liked Him Better Then

ISBN 978-0-89112-271-5

Printed in the United States of America

Cover design by Rick Gibson
Interior text design by Sandy Armstrong

Leafwood Publishers is an imprint of
Abilene Christian University Press
1626 Campus Court
Abilene, Texas 79601
1-877-816-4455 toll free

For current information about all Leafwood titles, visit our website:
www.leafwoodpublishers.com

11 12 13 14 15 16 / 7 6 5 4 3 2

To

Michelle, Tim, & Tom

who provided Myra and me such

JOY

as children and give us such

PRIDE

as adults

CONTENTS

Introduction

WHAT DOES *THAT* MEAN?

"Religion has often suffered from
the tendency to become parochial,
self-indulgent, self-seeking. . . . It has
often done more to canonize prejudices
than to wrestle for truth; to petrify the sacred
than to sanctify the secular."
—ABRAHAM HESCHEL

I Knew Jesus before He Was a Christian . . . and I Liked Him Better Then? What in the world is that supposed to mean?

The title is my way of bringing to the floor for discussion a critical truth about Jesus of Nazareth: the Jesus of history and the Jesus of common public perception are two very different persons. My claim is that the church has represented Jesus so poorly during the past two thousand years that his fundamental attractiveness as Savior has been lost to many, many people.

One of the most glaring ways the church has represented Jesus poorly is the way Christians are divided—into literally tens of thousands of denominations worldwide. The church has become laughable to the world—so laughable, in fact, that an online poll in 2005 named this joke from comic Emo Philips the "funniest religious joke ever."

> Once I saw this guy on a bridge about to jump. I said, "Don't do it!"
> He said, "Nobody loves me."
> I said, "God loves you. Do you believe in God?"
> He said, "Yes."
> I said, "Are you a Christian or a Jew?"
> He said, "A Christian."
> I said, "Me, too! Protestant or Catholic?"
> He said, "Protestant."
> I said, "Me, too! What franchise?"
> He said, "Baptist."
> I said, "Me, too! Northern Baptist or Southern Baptist?"
> He said, "Northern Baptist."
> I said, "Me, too! Northern Conservative Baptist or Northern Liberal Baptist?"
> He said, "Northern Conservative Baptist."
> I said, "Me, too! Northern Conservative Baptist Great Lakes Region, or Northern Conservative Baptist Eastern Region?"
> He said, "Northern Conservative Baptist Great Lakes Region."
> I said, "Me, too! Northern Conservative Baptist Great Lakes Region Council of 1879, or Northern Conservative Baptist Great Lakes Region Council of 1912?"
> He said, "Northern Conservative Baptist Great Lakes Region Council of 1912."
> I said, "Die, heretic!" And I pushed him over.[1]

As with much of the humor we create, the telling of Emo's story produces laughter because people identify with it. Just plug in your own denomination and one or two of its idiosyncratic beliefs, and you will get a true feel for it. At first I laughed and toyed with this story, relaying it to others; however, the laughter eventually gave way to a feeling of profound sadness.

This sadness comes from seeing the name of Jesus so tarnished and sullied across the centuries that many do not even recognize the difference between Jesus and the tarnished picture Christianity has painted over the years.

How did the name of Jesus suffer such devastating blows over time? How did we get to the point where Christianity has become an institution, a set of dogmas, and a barren ritual rather than being associated wholly with the actions of God in Christ and his teachings? If the church is to have a witness in the post-Pentecost, post-Constantine, postmodern twenty-first century, we need to take immediate action, but it should also be thoughtful action born out of sincere and authentic questioning of our own flaws.

In Philips's joke about the two confused men on the bridge, the important thing is being right—and proving that others aren't right. So the battle between church dogmas and rituals continues. And we wind up sounding like the little boy who declares, "My daddy can whip your daddy!" or pushing people off the bridge.

While Holy Scripture is quite clear on the identity and all-sufficiency of Christ as Savior, the things that produce the deep tribal divisions among followers of Christ are seldom all that fundamental. The divisions among Christians more often fall into the category of human interpretations and judgments that are put on par with the will of God.

This tendency of the human mind to blur the distinction between its judgments, on one hand, and the express commands of God, on the other, has bred both schism and bloodshed. Jesus quoted Isaiah on this point and rebuked what he called "teaching human precepts as doctrines"; in that same context, he went on to say that such a practice was anything but harmless and could result in "rejecting the commandment of God in order to keep your tradition" (Mark 7:6–9).

Jesus did not come to found a new religion that would generate still more human precepts masquerading as divine doctrine. He did not produce a creed or command us to write one. He came to "reveal the Father" and to declare that the kingdom rule of God is simultaneously "at hand" (i.e., nearby, available) and "among you" (i.e., already beginning to be realized, being witnessed in his ministry). Heaven knew that if we had an experience of God himself, we would never be the same. When Jesus appeared, people flocked to him—*until the power of religion turned against him and threatened them for giving the Son of Man an audience.*

In our own time and place, we still have a hard time grasping the critical truth that God is not a belief system, and salvation is not being right. According to Paul, the startling insight that has come to God-seekers at the end of their quest is not Gnostic-type epiphanies and secrets for the initiated. It is "Christ in you, the hope of glory" (Col. 1:27 NIV). Christ lives in his followers through our faith in him. It is just that simple—and just that complex.

In writing as early as that of the Ante-Nicene apologists for Christianity, much has been made of the parallels between Plato and Jesus. While some certainly exist, the two men are far more notable for their differences. For one, Plato thought the sure path to the meaning of life was a road of critical inquiry and self-examination that would end with an indescribable experience of The Good. For another, he believed the quest could be realized only as our true selves were freed from the burden and interference of our physical bodies. Thus, for example, Plato's famous "Allegory of the Cave."

Jesus, in contrast, taught that the meaning of human existence is much simpler. Males and females of the human race are embodied spirits—or inspirited bodies, if one prefers—who are called to be God's image-bearers to one another. Instead of flying away from our prison-bar mortal bodies, both spirit and body have been redeemed by God. Indeed, as Paul would later explain, a believer's body is not only inseparable from her spirit in life, but the body will be rejoined with the spirit forever in the resurrection. But there is more still: that same body is indwelt and transformed into a holy temple by the presence of the Holy Spirit.

Perhaps it was the medieval influence of the Neoplatonists on Christian theology that transformed much of church history into strife, division, damning judgment, and bloodshed. These arguments and wars have been over who is right and who is wrong, who is an insider to God's love and who is an outcast. A God whose heart is so tiny that it can embrace only those with intellects expansive enough to understand him and his mysteries isn't worthy of worship. We could only grovel in fear before a Monster Deity who would take delight in casting persons with flawed understanding into torment—no matter how earnestly those same people sought to find, understand, and follow him.

Jesus did not round up disciples to teach about the Trinity, millennium, baptismal formulas, worship protocols, head coverings, the Rapture, female clergy, or a thousand other topics that divide Christians today. He focused on the "fundamentals" instead. He gave his pupils their two-question final exam on the first day of the course—and left us our lifetimes to cram for it.

Question one: "Do you love God with heart, soul, mind, and strength?"

Question two: "Do you love your neighbor as you love yourself?"

I can imagine someone in the back of the lecture hall asking, "But aren't there more things that matter in this Life 101 course than those two questions?" And the answer comes back: "Everything that matters—every subtopic and footnote to the Law, Prophets, Psalms, Gospels, Letters, and Apocalypse—either flows from or leads to these two questions. Just work with them, and the rest will become clearer for you as we move through the course. So don't get distracted by the fine print."

But we do get distracted, often not by fine print but by our own religious slogans that steal our focus from Christ's final exam. These slogans often come in the form of bumper stickers. Dan Merchant's documentary film *Lord, Save Us from Your Followers* shows Merchant wearing a jumpsuit with dozens of bumper sticker slogans, from seriously religious to seriously silly.[2] While those he engaged may not have known what he was really after, they did give him what he was after: an incredible dialogue about faith. The aroma of Jesus is pleasant in the film, but many of the attitudes of his followers stink.

Merchant's documentary illustrates vividly what I want to discuss in depth in this book. People who read the Gospel stories from the life of Jesus are attracted to him. People who know Christ only through his followers often can't stand him. They cite the actions of his followers in explaining their rejection of him. They tell stories of rejection and hurt and immoral behavior done in the name of the Christian faith in order to explain their ranting and cursing at Jesus.

In the immediate aftermath of the devastating earthquake that hit Haiti on January 12, 2010, I was lamenting to a friend the fact that insurance policies and legal documents typically call such catastrophes "acts of God."

"Did you see the cartoon in the *Wall Street Journal* that showed God looking down on earth, telling an angel, 'Sunsets and cool breezes they take for granted, but floods and earthquakes they call Acts of God'?"

My friend thought about that for a moment, and I continued, tongue in cheek, "It appears to me God could use a good public relations firm to rehabilitate his image and reputation!"

My friend's comeback was unforgettable.

"I thought that was the church's job."

My friend is right. You and I are supposed to give people a positive impression of God. It is the church's business to be salt and light in the world, to draw the attention of people to God in a positive way.

In the next chapter, I want to probe deeper into the need to put Jesus in front of the church without diminishing the role of the church. Is it possible to be pro-Jesus and pro-church at the same time?

Chapter One

Pro-Jesus and Pro-Church

"The truth of the faith can be perceived only by doing a theology of Jesus Christ, and by redoing it over and over again."
—Karl Rahner

Can we be *pro-Jesus* and *pro-church*?

I am.

I am *pro-Jesus* and also *pro-church*.

Because it seems popular these days to exalt Jesus and simultaneously to bash the church, this statement will need some unpacking and clarification. One example of this kind of cultural thought is author Stephen King, who wrote, "And while I believe in God, I have no use for organized religion."[1]

Yes, I know. If Jesus and the church are understood biblically, King's statement is an utter impossibility. The church is the body and bride of Christ. One can't affirm the head and attack the body, be best friends with the groom and insult the bride he loves. You can't love the head and hack at the body. The body may need splints, stitches, or even major surgery at times. But it can't be severed from the head. You can't attack the body and affirm its head. They go together.

You and I may know all that, but our honest moments surely make us confess that we understand why other people would think otherwise.

They know enough about Jesus from the Gospels to believe there is a radical disconnect between him and the church they have experienced.

One man's experience is a perfect example of how the "churchified" Jesus can turn someone away from the Jesus of the Gospels.

Both of Lynn's parents were members of a small evangelical church in the inner city. His father was a deacon and superintendent of the Sunday school; he was often visible on the platform and could give an eloquent testimony about his love for Christ. Worship was a positive experience for Lynn. He wasn't particularly excited by the Bible studies on Sundays and Wednesdays. But he was there faithfully. The best part about the church classes was that he had formed some good friendships over time. So he was looking forward to entering eighth grade and excited about being part of some church events that were open only to full-fledged teens. He would be a teenager in a matter of four months.

The disconnect between Jesus and church became apparent to Lynn because of his alcoholic father. Visible and vocal as a Christian who received frequent affirmation from his church, Lynn's father was a holy terror at home. As he remembers it now, his father drank every night and was drunk most nights. The worst nights were the ones when his father had enough money to go to a bar and drink until he couldn't stand up, then he had to be picked up by Lynn's mother. Those nights were particularly awful, for he would come into the house screaming at his wife and slapping her. One night the slapping became a beating—a beating that left his wife in a coma and led to her death just after Lynn's first birthday as a teenager.

With his mother dead and his father in prison, Lynn was placed in a foster home. That home happened to be Jewish. There he found the stability he needed. He did reasonably well in school. When I met him, he was enrolled in a sophomore-level philosophy class I was teaching at a Christian college. He had volunteered to give a Jewish perspective on a topic we were discussing and had remained after class to talk. With a subtle grin, he said, "You seemed a bit surprised when I spoke up to say I was Jewish and offered the perspective of our rabbi on abortion. I take it you don't know many African Americans who are Jews."

Our conversation was relaxed and cordial as he told me about the turn in his life that caused him to embrace Judaism. "Look, I don't think every person who stands in front of a church to say he loves Jesus is the hypocrite my biological father is," he said. "And I have no reason to think you don't take your Christian faith seriously and live by it. But I had the words and forms of Christianity forced down my throat by a man who killed my mother and whose face I have vowed never to see again for as long as I live. Because of that man, I can't accept Christianity as true. It was a 'fake religion' in our house, and I won't have anything to do with it."

Lynn embraced Judaism because a Jewish family accepted him, loved him, nurtured him, and gave him positive options for living. The messengers became the message for Lynn, and that message looked far more godly and believable than the one that had come to him from his biological father. Haven't you heard that old cliché about preferring to see a sermon than to hear one? Broaden it a bit to say that Christianity, Islam, or atheism will gain more adherents by exhibiting basic virtue and compassion than through knock-down, drag-out arguments. Is the picture getting clearer now?

"Did you try to help him see the difference between his father's failure and the holy demands of the Christian faith? Did you tell him there are Jews who are alcoholics or thieves? Did you. . . ?" In that moment, I could only listen with a broken heart. It just wasn't a time for an argument. Interestingly, when I told him I was thinking about writing a book with the title *I Knew Jesus before He Was a Christian . . . and I Liked Him Better Then*, it was his turn to register a bit of surprise. When he wanted to know what the book would be about, I told him, and he got the point immediately—and gave me permission to tell his story in it.

We're still in touch and still talking. We understand each other clearly on the point that people can use church language and church structures to violate basic human dignity and negate the teachings of Jesus. Lynn knows far better than I the obstacle to faith that is put in someone's way when he or she experiences the phenomenon firsthand.

What Christianity Did to Jesus

First there was Jesus. Then there were his followers who made up the church, and they came to be called Christians. But these Christians tried to preserve the understanding of the true Jesus while doing damage to his cause and image at the same time.

Even so, Jesus is the original Christian. There is no such thing as Christianity apart from him. And the whole world needs to hear his claim to be the Way, the Truth, and the Life. "There is salvation in no one else [but Jesus]!" declared Peter—and I believe that. "God has given no other name under heaven by which we must be saved."

I believe Jesus Christ is not only the *monogenes* (i.e., unique and incomparable) Son of God but also the *monogenes* path that leads to God.

Jesus is an appealing and wonderful presence in the world. He brings hope and healing into broken lives. He gives sight to blind eyes and hearing to deaf ears. He brings lepers out of quarantine and back into their families, sinners out of banishment and back into community. He tells the people to whom nobody else will give the time of day that the kingdom of God belongs to them.

And yet *that* Jesus was so out of step with the religious establishment of his time that they murdered him—and have done so again and again across church history—to keep him from turning the masses away from their authority, buildings, rules and regulations, tithes and offerings, and the other trappings of institutionalized religion.

No sooner had Jesus come alive from the dead than Christianity came into being. Oh—it was actually a few generations later. From our vantage point of two thousand years, however, it was practically overnight. The young rebel of a rabbi who was so antiestablishment in teaching, lifestyle, and public perception was quickly transformed into the establishment himself.

His teaching became a checklist of orthodox doctrines rather than a series of enigmatic, multilayered parables. Those doctrines evolved into ever-finer hairsplitting that led to excommunication, the burning of heretics at the stake, and bloody wars in the name of the Prince of Peace. Christianity became the umbrella name for a host of competing denominational brands—Catholic and Protestant, Methodist and Baptist, Church of Christ and Nazarene, Pentecostal and Presbyterian.

American scholar Sam Pascoe is often credited with saying that Christianity was born in Israel, only to be taken to Greece and morphed into a philosophy. From there, it was taken to Rome and made into an institution of civil power. Eventually, it migrated to Europe where it was developed into a culture. Later still, it was brought to America and made into an entrepreneurial business enterprise.

That is the distinction I am making between the pre-Christianized Jesus and the Jesus morphed by two thousand years of history. The pre-Christianized Jesus has morphed into the Jesus of White Anglo-Saxon Protestantism, the Jesus of denominational rivalry and political partisanship, the Jesus who tolerates the hypocrisy Lynn experienced in a family setting, the Jesus who is known for those he condemns to hell and judges unworthy of his company, the Jesus who defines people by their theology and church membership.

The Problem Is Not New

Ironically and tragically, misrepresenting God is not a problem unknown to religious history before Christianity. The faith and life envisioned in the Hebrew Bible degenerated to a religion we typically call Judaism by the time Jesus came among humankind. And the two were as fundamentally different as I am claiming the faith and life modeled by Jesus for his followers and institutionalized Christianity to be in our time.

To illustrate this, I want to tell a story from the life of Christ and then give you some background for how God's original intention can get seriously distorted among believers and godly people. It is a parable from Jesus' lips about how religion can sometimes be a barrier between a man or woman and God. Here is the story Jesus told:

> Two men went into the temple to pray. One was a Pharisee and the other a tax collector. The Pharisee stood over by himself and prayed, "God, I thank you that I am not greedy, dishonest, and unfaithful in marriage like other people. And I am really glad that I am not like that tax collector over there. I go without eating for two days a week, and I give you one tenth of all I earn." The tax collector stood off at a distance and did not think he was good enough even to look up toward heaven. He was so sorry for what he had done that he pounded his chest and prayed, "God, have pity on me! I am such a sinner."
>
> Then Jesus said, "When the two men went home, it was the tax collector and not the Pharisee who was pleasing to God. If you put yourself above others, you will be put down. But if you humble yourself, you will be honored." (Luke 18:10–14 CEV)

First, don't be too hard on the Pharisee in this story. He is a creation of his environment. It could have been someone living in "all good conscience"—as Saul, the Pharisee from Tarsus, had for all of his pre-Damascus-road life. The Pharisee was a conservative. He held a high view of Scripture. There is no reason to think he didn't love Yahweh. It is just that he had gone to church—pardon me, temple and synagogue—all his life. And he had paid attention. He had been taught that God's favor depends on what you do and don't do. So you tithe, fast, and stay with your family. You certainly don't cheat people, think money is the most important thing in your life, or live as an outcast to God-fearing people. Thus he attended synagogue, learned to pray in the customary way, memorized key passages from the Bible, protected his reputation by avoiding bad company, and likely had the respect of everybody in his community.

Second, don't make the tax collector in this story to be heroically righteous. All indications are that we are to see him in Jesus' story the way everybody saw such people in Jewish society of that time. He was from the lower class of society. His very profession of collecting Roman coins in payment for the empire's tax coffers made him unclean. Uncleanness aside, he belonged to an identifiable social class that included prostitutes, thieves, gamblers, shepherds, and loan sharks. These "low class" folk were seen as living by preying on the weaknesses of others. Prostitutes preyed on passion, gamblers and loan sharks on greed, and shepherds on the lands and flocks of others. Tax collectors were regarded as "official thieves" because their job of deciding how much tax or toll money someone paid was their decision—with a commission added. It was a job made for dishonest people, and most of the people who gravitated to it likely were deceitful cheats.

So let me recast the parable in contemporary terms.

> Two men went to church on a Sunday morning. One was a deacon and the other a closet homosexual. The deacon called the service to order and prayed, "God, I thank you that we are a strong and growing church that is unashamed to take a stand on abortion, X-rated movies, and divorce. We fear for our country, Lord, with all the blatant homosexuality being glamorized in the media and defended by our politicians. I'm truly grateful for the youth ministry here and that you have taught us to be generous enough to send our teens to help rebuild a school in quake-ravaged Haiti."
>
> Meanwhile, the gay man was sitting toward the back of the sanctuary and didn't think he was good enough even to join in

> the prayer. He was so miserable over the conflicts in his heart and life that he could only whisper, as a tear rolled down his cheek, "God, have pity on me! I am such a sinner."
>
> Then Jesus said, "When the two men went home that day, it was the homosexual and not the deacon who was pleasing to God. If you put yourself above others, you will be put down. But if you humble yourself, you will be honored."

In Jesus' ministry, he paid attention to the poor and hungry, the lame and blind, the leprous and demon-possessed, the widows and orphans. Collectively, the Gospels refer to them as "the masses" or "the little ones." He didn't sing invitation songs, but he did extend dinner invitations—to tax collectors, notorious sinners, prostitutes, and people living together without a marriage document. Then we would need to lengthen the list to add those despised Samaritan dogs, Roman soldiers, and other hated classes. Collectively, the Pharisees (see John 7:49) lumped people such as these into a class they deemed "ignorant of the law" and damned (i.e., "God's curse is on them!").

They weren't welcome at temple or synagogue. They were left off the dinner lists of the community's best people—certainly those of the clergy and Bible scholars. They were the people parents pointed out to their children and—in voices loud enough to be heard—told them to avoid and fear. They were the lepers, crippled, poor, and orphaned that the children themselves often felt free to torment by mocking their crooked frames, running up to spit on them, or pelting them with rocks. They were shut out and hopeless. They were life's losers and religion's outsiders.

Even if a prostitute or tax collector repented and wanted to make atonement by means of a temple sacrifice, that would cost money. But you weren't allowed to use tainted money gotten by prostitution or the collection of taxes to pay for the ritual. So you were doubly damned—damned by your sin and damned by your inability to be made clean. To be a "sinner" was your fate. It was God's will and unchangeable.

Jesus and Outsiders

Yet Jesus entered the world of losers, outcasts, and sinners consciously and deliberately. He let himself be made unclean by being touched by a hemorrhaging woman and then reaching out to touch a leper and a blind man. Why, he even touched dead people. He went into a tax collector's home. He ate with people in public places with the full knowledge that doing so made him an outcast along with them.

"When he saw the crowds, he had compassion on them because they were confused and helpless, like sheep without a shepherd" (Matt. 9:36 NLT). "A man with leprosy came and knelt in front of Jesus, begging to be healed. 'If you are willing, you can heal me and make me clean,' he said. Moved with compassion, Jesus reached out and touched him. 'I am willing,' he said. 'Be healed!'" (Mark 1:40–41 NLT). In the Parable of the Good Samaritan—a story whose shocking nature we just seem not to grasp—a "despised Samaritan" is the hero who shows mercy; so a Samaritan becomes the answer to a Jewish man's request for Jesus to tell him who his neighbor is (Luke 10:25–37).

This Jesus is saving people, but he is doing it as an "outsider" to establishment religiosity. This Jesus reads the Prophets in synagogue as a "lay reader," but he is not "clergy." This Jesus creates chaos in the temple compound by shooing birds and freeing animals—as well as turning over the tables of the moneychangers. We know full well that Jesus didn't fit Judaism's institutional mold. He was a rebel and a maverick. On the same day, he would make Pharisees, Sadducees, and Herodians all mad at him! But we like that Jesus. He is the anti-Judaism Jew who is nonetheless the Christ, the Son of the Living God.

So tell me, do you really think Jesus fits Christianity's institutional mold any better than he fit the one Judaism offered him? Which denomination do you think he would join today? Or do you think he just might not choose to be part of any of our churches—mainline, evangelical, nondenominational, or otherwise?

I fear he could look at all of us and say, "I never knew *any* of your churches!"

The ongoing sex-abuse scandal in Catholicism, unending televangelist impieties among Protestants, ungodly rants by racists and homophobes, hypocrisy in local churches, gossip among workers in Christian ministry, judgmental posturing—these are the things that make people anti-church.

But these are not the actions sanctioned for Christ's body. They are its misbehaviors and malfunctions! Such inept activities are the body of Christ only to the degree that a cancerous mass is my body. It is growing there. It is being nourished by certain bodily systems. But a cancer is—by definition—an aberrant, intrusive, life-threatening growth within one's body. It subverts and undermines health. The threat is that it can destroy the body's very life.

To press the cancer metaphor a bit further, the Body of Christ has accumulated so many of these noxious growths across the centuries that it is positively deformed and unattractive. Even where surgery and rehabilitation have been attempted, the scars are ugly and the memories painful. But the appropriate treatment at this point is hardly *decapitation*. Beheading is not a therapeutic blow but a murderous assault.

Even so, people can't destroy the church that is Christ's body. A great deal of the ambivalence about the church these days may be summed up in an anecdote a nonconfessing friend shared with me. During a frustrating argument with a Roman Catholic Cardinal, Napoleon Bonaparte supposedly burst out: "Your eminence, are you not aware that I have the power to destroy the Catholic Church?" According to the story, the Cardinal made this rueful response: "Your Majesty, we, the clergy, have done our best to destroy the church for the last 1700 years. We have not succeeded, and neither will you."

After all, people have declared the demise of the church repeatedly over the past two millennia. It has proved more durable than anyone thought. Whether at the hands of friend or foe, it has been severely ill-treated and abused. In the words of an old hymn by Samuel J. Stone:

> Though with a scornful wonder
> we see her sore oppressed,
> by schisms rent asunder,
> by heresies distressed,
> yet saints their watch are keeping;
> their cry goes up, "How long?"
> And soon the night of weeping
> shall be the morn of song.[2]

Still, the church is breathing and functioning and doing positive, life-transforming things that we will explore later in the book. For now, however, I want to work with another metaphor to help explain the ideal relationship between Christ and the church.

Think now of marriage, family, and home. After all, another biblical image of the relationship between Christ and the church is to liken it to the bond between husband and wife. Interestingly, both the body-to-head and bride-to-groom figures of speech trace to the same New Testament writer, Paul (see Rom. 12:4–5; Eph. 5:31).

Have there been suggestions that marriage should be abolished? Many. Have there been justifiable criticisms of family dysfunction, abuse, and harm? Certainly. But the consensus opinion across time seems clearly to be against the wholesale abolition of home and family. Instead, we remind ourselves that the ideal of loving adults who create and nurture children to maturity in a context of emotional security is sound. It is obviously and fundamentally a good idea. The fact that so many marriages fail or that some marriages are authoritarian and abusive does not argue against the legitimacy—even desirability—of healthy family units.

To the contrary, I assume that most couples who make a free and loving choice to say "I do" have the same intention my wife and I had when we got married. We believed we would not have to follow a predetermined path to inevitable failure. We determined to continue loving each other, no matter what might come our way. We promised to work through our problems. We gave our word to be faithful companions "in sickness and in health, in good times and in bad, until death do us part, so help us God." And we've made it—this far! So have many, many others.

Thus, in spite of the fact that some people have had such bad experiences in love and marriage that they have given up on both, most of us keep trying to do it right. At least, we keep trying to do better at it than we may have witnessed. We might even confess that we are trying to do it better now than we were able to do it at some earlier time. But we haven't denounced love or marriage or family—in spite of all the problems and bitter disappointments associated with them.

Thus Says the Lord: "Stop Embarrassing Me!"

Back then to the original point of this chapter: One can be both pro-Jesus and pro-church. But the order is important in both cases—Jesus *first*, and then the church.

Putting Jesus "first" here is a matter of priority rather than mere sequence. Just as some people already married have had to learn how to love one another, so some church members may yet need to discover, fall in love with, and experience the fullness of Christ. While the ideal is that one know Christ and thus be constituted a part of his church, the reality is that many become church members only to wind up spiritually empty and disillusioned; their urgent need is to discover that knowing Jesus is so much more than being a church member.

Indeed, the theological priorities here are critical—Jesus over church, head directing body, organic health valued above institutional structures. The mistake of our time and place in history is both bifurcation (i.e., separation of Jesus from church) and reversal of priorities (i.e., allowing church as we have experienced it to define Jesus and to substitute for our experience of him).

The movie *Oh, God!* has John Denver in the role of a nondescript supermarket manager who is recruited to hear God and to communicate his message to skeptical hearers. In the sometimes-irreverent dialogue, there are also sometimes-insightful moments about religion in the modern setting. The voice of God, supplied by George Burns, gives Denver messages to deliver that sometimes smack of the prophetic.

In one scene, for example, Denver's character is at a religious service where an evangelist is holding forth—in caricature, of course. Denver interrupts the preacher to inform him that God has a special message just for him. So the evangelist makes the mistake of stopping the service, focusing the attention of the crowd, and telling everyone, "This young man has come with a message from God."

John Denver looks at the preacher with laser-like focus and delivers his message: "God wants you to shut up because you're embarrassing him!"

Could that be the message of God to some of us who have dared to preach? To whole denominations about our theologies? To a given church about its ministry to the community where God has placed it? One needs only to read the Old Testament prophets to hear Yahweh thunder his disapproval of faithless priests and false prophets to know that it *could* happen. One needs only to read the newspaper to know it *does* happen.

It is possible for the administrative, institutional, and visible-spokesperson roles in the contemporary church to be so filled with phonies that what presents itself to the world as Christ's body actually turns the world against Christ Jesus himself. I believe this helps explain why so many people today declare themselves "spiritual" but resist the designation "religious." It has to be part of the reason the largest percentage growth in surveys of "religious affiliation" over the past couple of decades has been neither Baptist nor Roman Catholic nor nondenominational, but "none." The church body has become not only an *embarrassment* to its Jesus-head, but also a significant *obstacle* to redemption for those who need and otherwise would be attracted to Jesus.

This book claims that unbelievers would be better served by focusing on Jesus rather than on his followers. Since that is unrealistic, though, my challenge is that the church must get its act together to major on "righteousness and peace and joy in the Holy Spirit" rather than "food and drink [regulations]" (see Rom. 14:17) or "church growth [projects]" or "building and grounds [fundraisers]."

Until church is more than institutional maintenance, self-serving programs, and a voting bloc to be courted by candidates for public office, it has no more right to offer itself as Christ's representative in the world than a philandering husband has the right to present himself as the spokesman-model for marital fidelity.

Or, said positively, only when the church becomes the dispenser of righteousness, peace, and joy will it actually have the right to claim identity as the body of Christ. Only when it models and dispenses faith, hope, and love will it have any credibility for further discussion.

A Long-Standing Problem for the Church

This isn't a new problem for the Christian community. "Religion that is pure and undefiled before God, the Father, is this: to care for orphans and widows in their distress, and to keep oneself unstained by the world" (James 1:27). Why the stress on "pure" and "undefiled" as descriptors for religion? Do you think James, the half-brother of Jesus, saw a distinction between what was passing as "religion" and authentic, God-affirming "spirituality" in his day? And this was written only about fifteen years after the Pentecost birthday of the church.

Following is an expressive paraphrase of this same section of Scripture. "Anyone who sets himself up as 'religious' by talking a good game is self-deceived. This kind of religion is hot air and only hot air. Real religion, the kind that passes muster before God the Father, is this: Reach out to the homeless and loveless in their plight, and guard against corruption from the godless world" (James 1:26–27 MSG). In other words, let *compassion* and *holiness* identify you and commend your faith to others—not your church membership, your theological hairsplitting, or your scathing judgments of others.

Back before church membership was an issue, the one who was Immanuel—God with us—showed his would-be followers how to treat people and so to receive the kingdom of heaven.

The goal of this book is to distinguish the two and to offer the latter as not only more desirable and more attractive, but also as a real possibility for our place and time. In the following chapter, I want to address a problem that has been around for 1700 years—one we cannot not keep covering up or ignoring.

Chapter Two

THE CHURCH OF SANCTIFIED RELIGIOSITY

"It is far too easy for us to base our claims to God on our own Christian religiosity and our church commitment, and in so doing utterly to misunderstand and distort the Christian idea."
—DIETRICH BONHOEFFER

Perhaps you have seen the movie *Chocolat*. It tells a story that bears directly on the thesis of this book—and could provide a handle to grasp for anyone who is still trying to figure out how one can distinguish between Jesus and Christianity.

I teach a college course for freshmen practically every semester. I sometimes require that they see *Chocolat* for the sake of either an essay or class discussion about attitudes toward religion. It is quite the appropriate parable for contrasting religion and spirituality. It paints a distinctly negative and—so most students seem to think—accurate picture of institutional church. To say the least, there are different presentations of spirituality in the film that reflect our culture's take on things. The church in the movie happens to be Roman Catholic, but that is incidental to the story. People from Methodist, Pentecostal, and Community Churches have all claimed to know the church in *Chocolat* by some direct experience.

The film opens in a small French village, and the camera captures a dull, flowerless town square. The intimidating mayor of the town, the Comte de Reynaud, controls the churchgoing people by his authoritarian manner. His goal is to enforce a rigid moral order, maintain the village's traditional ways, and see to it that "tranquility" is undisturbed. Relationships are strained and frayed. Then the movie's heroine, Vianne, and her young daughter appear—"blown in by a sly wind from the north" and wearing colorful red capes. In the season of Lent, Vianne rents an old pastry shop, renovates it, and opens a chocolaterie. The action begins as the sweet chocolates not only induce smiles but seem to invigorate the very lives of the townspeople.

To take only one case study from the movie, a couple—Josephine and Serge—run the town's café. Their relationship is abysmal. The drunken Serge abuses his wife, and Josephine steals occasionally just to have something in her life that is her own and under her control. Vianne serves delicious chocolate to a cowering Josephine, befriends her, and eventually employs her in the shop; Josephine flourishes in the new context of acceptance and empowerment.

Josephine's newly discovered sense of identity quickly becomes a threat to Serge. He doesn't know what to do with a wife who does something other than cringe before his threats. He certainly doesn't have a clue about what to do when she leaves him. So he goes to the Comte who proposes to rehabilitate Serge with lectures, discipline, and a new wardrobe. You likely do not need to see the movie to figure out which approach works for real change—acceptance or judgment, empowering love or debilitating censure, freedom to grow or tight-at-the-neck collars. The same contrast plays out among various characters in the film.

In a climactic moment at the end of *Chocolat*, the village's young priest stands before his congregation to say, "We must measure our goodness, not by what we don't do, what we deny ourselves, or whom we exclude. Instead, we should measure ourselves by what we embrace, what we create, and whom we include."[1]

It is a parable about two paths to rebuilding broken lives. Sadly, the story grounds Vianne's open, affirming view of life in her Mayan roots—not in Jesus. Perhaps the latter option did not appear realistic to the author. From a Christian background, however, it doesn't require much mental adjustment to see the film as a symbol of two very different approaches to faith. One is authoritarian and rigid, seeking to have an impact on its environment from a hostile posture and with primary emphasis on form, custom, and attendance; its alternative is compassionate and engaging, working via a network of acceptance, gentle nurture, and transformation over time. In their book *The Shaping of Things to Come*, Frost and Hirsch use Vianne's chocolaterie as their "vision of an incarnational church."

> She is warm, nonjudgmental and compassionate, offering grace and peace to the troubled community. Her shop is a haven, but she doesn't simply wait for people to enter. She engages the lives and troubles of her community and offers practical help as well as space for honesty and truthtelling to happen. She celebrates life, good food (Armande's [her landlady who is alienated from her daughter] seventieth birthday party includes a devilishly exotic menu), loud laughter, love, romance, storytelling, fantasy, and imagination. In fact, Armande's birthday party reminded us of Matthew's party for Jesus (Mark 2:15) where the outcasts, sinners, and tax collectors celebrated with the Messiah. Like Jesus, Vianne has collected the outcasts, the misfits, and created a veritable feast in their honor.[2]

In this chapter, let's explore some of the fundamental distinctions that would follow from an institutional religiosity on the one hand versus the fresh breath of the Holy Spirit on the other, an approach to church as of the status quo versus church as the corporate expression of Christ's presence in the world that liberates and empowers people to embrace an abundant life.

1700 Years of Failure

If I were to make the following statement, many people would be shocked, and some would think me heretical: *Church as it has been done for the past 1700 years has failed profoundly and needs to be abandoned*. (Millions, of course, have already done just that. They've abandoned the church and have no intention of ever returning to it.) Let me explain why I think the statement is true—but why I don't think we should give up entirely on the idea of church. I believe we need to abandon what I have called "institutionalized religiosity" or "institutional church" for the sake of experiencing a relational faith that can be lived as authentic spirituality.

For the past 1700 years, people have been saddled with a *form* (i.e., institutional church complete with power brokers) and a *formula* (i.e., doctrinal tenets that had to be proved by complicated reasoning that most couldn't grasp but were afraid to challenge for fear of being thrown out of the institution by one of the power brokers) that don't work well at all. Catholics have done it, and Protestants have, too. Baptists have been bad at it, and so have Churches of Christ. It's everywhere! And the marvel of it all is that God has been working through those flawed forms and incoherent formulas to reach people, save people, and transform people.

One of the great strengths of Christianity has been its ability to endure, accommodate, and use the cultural shifts across centuries without losing its essence. Even in its most perverted and misguided forms, the Christian religion has continued to pass around a central message about Jesus' death, burial, and resurrection. And there have been people in the most abysmal of churches in the most corrupt of cultures who have been counted among the great host of the redeemed. They are people in a church Jesus can pronounce "dead," yet he still promises them their names are in the Book of Life (see Rev. 3:1–6). They have been given (i.e., graced with) divine favor on account of God's great love and in spite of church inadequacies or personal failures. Even some who have been kicked out of churches were made more vitally engaged in the kingdom of God for their sufferings—whether Luther or Tyndale or countless other individuals, families, or groups whose names are unknown to us but precious to Christ.

The Church of Modernity

Over the past five hundred years, a particular form of institutional church that has functioned variously as a club, nation-state, forensic society, and irrelevance has obscured the presence and activity of God. Though claiming to be "scientific" by putting the Bible under an intellectual microscope in order to find the essential theological facts buried in its pages, this church was more often "juridical" in its function. By applying various systems of "objective interpretation of the Bible," the persons who functioned as power broker-judges within the system would include or exclude applicants.

With clear doctrinal formulations, the Church of Modernity proclaimed the gospel story in terms of laws, steps, creedal statements, and confessions. There was little tolerance for leaving anything unexplained and even less tolerance for persons who did not hail the explanation offered—contrived as it might have been—as conclusive. The Christian faith was termed a "system," and one's place within that system was determined by an all-or-nothing attitude toward it.

The Modern Church stressed discipleship that showed itself principally in Bible study, memorization of Scripture, and doctrinal correctness. Many people could not help noticing that some of the best teachers who could quote the most verses were at times the grumpiest, meanest, and least-liked people in their nonchurch worlds of extended family, neighborhood, and workplace.

A key word used often in this historical version of church was *autonomy*. When agreement on some fine point of doctrine was not attained, individuals and groups felt free to break off and further fragment the body for the sake of maintaining doctrinal purity. Thus came the formation of literally hundreds of denominations and nondenominations, with each group believing that unity could be restored when and only when the other group renounced its error and embraced the "right" interpretation of this or that point.

Is this survey of 1700 years of Christian history grossly oversimplified? Absolutely. But is it fundamentally correct in outlining the influence of Constantine in reducing the church from the countercultural people of God into a culture-copying institution? I believe it is. Is it fundamentally accurate in describing how the church has functioned on a pseudoscientific template in the period beginning with the Enlightenment until now? Again, I believe it is.

Let me repeat that the gospel is both other than and greater than any cultural impediments to its ability to reach, capture, and redeem people. It got through the layers of legalistic religion in Jerusalem in the first century. It penetrated the moral and philosophic bankruptcy of Greek thought in Athens, Corinth, and Rome. And it was the source of hope and salvation to thousands upon thousands in the medieval and modern periods of history that have followed.

But the fact remains that Christians of every generation and geographic placement, from every background and belief, with whatever cultural baggage or advantage should ask ourselves about God's will for us as we await Christ's return. What does he want us to be doing in our time and place? Are there obstacles to the gospel that we need to remove? Are there better ways to live and teach the gospel than we have used to date? Or, if we shift the question farther from ourselves and more to God himself, perhaps we should ask this: What options is God opening to those who love him? What things is he trying to teach us? What opportunities has he created for communicating the gospel to people in our time?

"I Will Build My Church"

Here is the conversation that began all our ongoing conversations about church:

> When Jesus came to the region of Caesarea Philippi, he asked his disciples, "Who do people say the Son of Man is?"
>
> They replied, "Some say John the Baptist; others say Elijah; and still others, Jeremiah or one of the prophets."
>
> "But what about you?" he asked. "Who do you say I am?"
>
> Simon Peter answered, "You are the Christ, the Son of the living God."
>
> Jesus replied, "Blessed are you, Simon son of Jonah, for this was not revealed to you by man, but by my Father in heaven. And I tell you that you are Peter, and on this rock I will build my church, and the gates of Hades will not overcome it. I will give you the keys of the kingdom of heaven; whatever you bind on earth will be bound in heaven, and whatever you loose on earth will be loosed in heaven." Then he warned his disciples not to tell anyone that he was the Christ. (Matt. 16:13–20 NIV)

It is impossible to say exactly what Jesus had in mind when he promised to build his church. Whatever "ideal" he envisioned, we know the church only as flawed reality. The Jerusalem church was not a diverse community, had trouble dealing with the conversion of Samaritans and Gentiles, and had its own holdover problems from the flawed practice of Judaism on which it based its understandings and practices. It wasn't that much better, if at all, among the Gentile churches at Thessalonica, at Corinth, or in the region of Galatia. All these churches had serious issues with importing either the Greek philosophies or the pagan lifestyles of their cultures into the church.

Or maybe what I've just said about Jesus and his expectations for church is mistaken. Perhaps he knew that the church he promised to build would be exactly as it turned out to be. Maybe he never envisioned that it would be flawless in doctrine and virtuous in lifestyle. It just might be that he promised to build a church where men and women with imperfect understanding, compromised reputation, and limited potential would form a community of love, accountability, and nurture where gradual spiritual transformation would take place among people over time. That, in fact, is what I suspect he was promising. We have imported our expectations of perfection and imposed our notions of what ought to be so onto the divine intention.

A church leader attended a seminar several years ago at which I made a version of the point I've just registered about the church as "a community of love, accountability, and nurture where gradual spiritual transformation would take place among people over time." He expressed a degree of confusion over what I was saying. He insisted he'd never seen church function except on a corporation model of budgets, committees, and boards. He named the city and state from which he had come and asked me to refer him to the closest church I knew that was functioning as the sort of body I thought a church ought to be. In the quick exchange of a question-and-answer session, I told him that the best thing for him might be to attend Alcoholics Anonymous for three months to get a glimpse of what I thought the church was like in its earliest days—and needed to recapture.

I've given a similar response to that same question on dozens of occasions. So I didn't recognize the man or remember our exchange when I saw him almost two years after that day. He introduced himself, reminded me of our exchange, and said, "I took your advice. And it has revolutionized my thinking—and turned me into a crusader among my fellow-elders! I've got the other four elders of our church attending AA with me, and we are beginning to understand how to shepherd our little flock of about 250 people."

He proceeded to tell me that he went to that first twelve-step meeting with a lot of apprehension. After all, he wasn't an alcoholic. As he went into the open meeting, he almost balked because he wasn't among "his kind." Some had huge beer bellies. Some had wild tattoos. Several were smoking, some were cursing, and a few were just downright scary looking! But he saw some from the suit-and-tie crowd there, too. He risked it. Didn't say a word for the first several meetings. And eventually he became convinced there was something special at work in those Thursday meetings.

He gradually began to sit somewhere other than the darkest and most remote corner of the room. And since twelve-step groups involve vulnerability, he began to be offered things from people's life histories that nobody had ever trusted to him before. They were telling him about drinking binges and lost jobs, marital infidelities and fights, nights in the drunk tank and waking up in places they didn't remember going to the night before. Before long, he was sensing a need to participate himself. For the first time in his adult life, he told somebody about being sexually molested as a child. He poured out his heart to about two dozen people—who cried, put their arms around him, asked understanding questions, and told him they would help him work through his anguish. A couple of other men in the group told of similar experiences.

A group within the group now, they have met to tell their stories in greater detail, vent the outrage that they couldn't voice as children, and give each other reassurance. They've read a couple of books and discussed them. They have been especially helpful to one another with the feelings of shame they had been carrying for all these years. He says they are thinking about forming a support group for male survivors of sexual assault. "By the way," he said, "I understand now why you told me to go to Alcoholics Anonymous to get a glimpse of what church should be. I've got it now! And I'll never be the same 'company man' I was for so many years in the church."

Alcoholics Anonymous owns no meeting properties and has no headquarters. Nobody speaks for it. There are no officers. No dues. No penalties—except to your recovery—for missing meetings. Meetings aren't uniform in size or length or focus. And the requirement for membership—there is no formal "membership" in AA—is a desire to get sober. To have your life back from addiction to alcohol. To be able to have a sane relationship with God and with the people who matter to you.

An Amazing Community of Faith

The church you read about in the book of Acts must have looked and functioned more like an AA meeting than any church you ever wanted to join. Christians met in small groups in one another's homes. Sunday was a regular meeting day, but they were getting together every day somewhere. They ate together—often consecrating their meal and conversation and relationship by simple words and prayers over bread and wine in memory of Christ. Occasionally word would spread among all the groups as best they knew to communicate with one another about a "big meeting" with a speaker to exhort them all to faithfulness. But the heart of that church beat in those house churches.

That church didn't own property or build buildings for two or three hundred years after Jesus established it. It had no headquarters. No dues. The people it called "officers" —probably usually for a city or region rather than for just one house church—were essentially being designated as mature examples to the groups of believers who needed counsel and teaching. There was a spirit of community and bonding among its members. Outsiders are known to have commented, "Look how those 'Christ followers' love one another and look out for each other!" You could hear a touch of envy in the voices of some of them as they said it.

> All the believers met together constantly and shared everything they had. They sold their possessions and shared the proceeds with those in need. They worshiped together at the Temple each day, met in homes for the Lord's Supper, and shared their

meals with great joy and generosity—all the while praising God and enjoying the goodwill of all the people. And each day the Lord added to their group those who were being saved. (Acts 2:44–47 NLT)

The church became such a phenomenon that both religious and political leaders of the first and second centuries began persecuting it. Opposition and social isolation did nothing but make the Christians closer to one another. Finally, in the early fourth century, Emperor Constantine adopted an if-I-can't-beat-them-I'll-join-them attitude toward the church. And that was the beginning of the church's fateful decline. He made the loosely associated house churches into land-owning, building-filling church members. But land and buildings needed managers, so a professional class of paid clergy arose. It was no time until bigger-is-better came to be the rule for these institutional churches, and the leaders of the larger churches had more prestige and clout than the ones with only a handful of people.

The loving family of God had been prostituted into a competitive enterprise. The organism morphed into an organization. And the corporate expression of Jesus' presence in the world turned into a religious corporation.

The institutional church increasingly allied itself with power instead of with the weak, vulnerable, and oppressed. Spiritual work was done by carnal means—from "converting" people through war to "worshipping" via ritual nobody understood to "ministering" through impersonal give-aways to people with whom nobody wanted to spend time. The simple church of love, accountability, and nurture became a complex set of doctrines, rituals, and hierarchies. God got lost in the process!

"Religionless Christianity"

One of the people who witnessed the loss of God and saw Christianity negate the presence and power of Jesus was Dietrich Bonhoeffer. While I am no Bonhoeffer scholar, I am convinced that the co-opting of his phrase "religionless Christianity" by later liberal theologians of the God-is-dead movement[3] seriously misinterprets him.

The story of Bonhoeffer's martyrdom during the awful Nazi era in Germany is too well-known to need repeating here. He saw the state church come under the influence of National Socialism and sell its soul to a spirit that was anti-God because of its anti-human genocide. He knew the biblical text that says anyone who professes love for the God he has not seen while hating the fellow-humans he encounters is a liar. Hitler's anti-Semitism was sometimes overtly embraced and affirmed by German theologians and churches—much as hatred against another race was preached from pulpits in pre-Civil War America and during the era of South African apartheid. More often still, it was covertly embraced through the silence of theologians, clergy, and churchgoing citizens who did nothing either to oppose Hitler or to assist Jews, homosexuals, or others who were on the Nazi list of "undesirables."

Well before the Nazis came to power and long before he coined the term "religionless Christianity," Bonhoeffer had made a distinction between the true genius of Christian faith and the corrupted practices of what he called "Christian religiosity." In a presentation he made as a twenty-two-year-old, he made the point to which he would return as a mature theologian.

> With that we have articulated a basic criticism of the most grandiose of all human attempts to advance toward the divine—by way of the church. Christianity conceals within itself a germ hostile to the church. It is far too easy for us to base our claims to God on our own Christian religiosity and our church commitment, and in so doing utterly to misunderstand and distort the Christian idea.[4]

In the passing of time and while witnessing (and suffering from!) the failures of Germany's institutional Christianity, Bonhoeffer pleaded passionately for the lordship of Christ over not only the church but all human experience and enterprise. He saw and objected to Christianity that had become formulaic and contained in Sunday assemblies and chose instead to voice and to live a confession of Christ that would cost him his life. Surely many of us who have read his *Life Together* or *The Cost of Discipleship* have done so without appreciating the full-throat outcry they represent against not just a political and social regime (i.e., Hitler and National Socialism) but also the failed church of his time and place.

Eric Metaxas interprets Bonhoeffer as someone who would be labeled an advocate for "missional church" or "incarnational faith" in our time. An understanding of God as the one who deals with humanity's private fears or intellectual mysteries would have satisfied him then no more than it satisfies the "nones" of today's spiritual-but-not-religious culture. On the interpretation of Metaxas, the German theologian was not wondering about the irrelevance of Jesus to the bleak situation of his time but the impotence of religion as it was functioning in that dark hour. He explains in *Bonhoeffer*:

> What Bonhoeffer meant by "religion" was not true Christianity, but the ersatz and abbreviated Christianity that he spent his life working against. This "religious" Christianity had failed Germany and the West during this great time of crisis, for one thing, and he wondered whether it wasn't finally time for the lordship of Jesus Christ to move past Sunday mornings and churches and into the whole world. But this was simply an extension of his previous theology, which was dedicatedly Bible centered and Christ centered. . . .
>
> Bonhoeffer was thinking in a new way about what he had been thinking and saying for two decades: God was bigger than everyone imagined, and he wanted more of his followers and more of the world than was given him. Bonhoeffer recognized

> that standard-issue "religion" had made God small, having dominion only over those things we could not explain. That "religious" God was merely the "God of the gaps," the God who concerned himself with our "secret sins" and hidden thoughts. But Bonhoeffer rejected this abbreviated God. . . . Bonhoeffer was wondering if it wasn't time to bring God into the whole world and stop pretending he wanted only to live in those religious corners we reserved for him.[5]

Isn't that question worth asking in every generation? To the degree that our religions have made God small, we must affirm him in his fullness. To the degree that we have confined the Holy Spirit to the Bible or to Sunday morning, we must plead for him to blow fresh wind or—if necessary—to pour fresh fire into our midst. To the degree that our take on being a Christian is tame and insulated from life, we must follow Jesus to a life that is bold and integrated into all of life.

The Beginnings of Renewal

Organized religiosity has failed. Institutional church is dead as an effective means for representing God to the emerging scene. This stiff-and-stilted church needs to become more relational, hungrier for the Truth, and open to the Spirit. It *is* time for the lordship of Jesus Christ to move past Sunday mornings, away from rigid formulas, and out of church buildings. It is time for believers to see ourselves as missionaries to our own places—not going there to rant, judge, or speak, but to live as Christ's representatives who connect with people for the sake of being God-presence to them. Be part of the neighborhood. Sit at a table with people to listen to their stories. Speak the *shalom* of righteousness, joy, and peace into their lives. Ask God to show you the time for speaking and sharing your experience of Jesus to them. Then expect the Spirit of God to move in his time and by his power to bring conviction, offer hope, and give redemption.

In contrast to many of Christianity's "programs" that make "prospects" of people and "projects" of neighborhoods or cities, follow the model of Jesus to enflesh the gospel faithfully, love people unselfishly, and build community that is authentic. Nurture your own life through the spiritual disciplines of prayer and Scripture reading, as well as suffering and learning endurance; otherwise, you will burn out. Then ask God to lead you into situations where you can break down barriers and build up people.

Does that sound like a world where committees, budgets, and size are priorities? Does it smack of intrusive presence and judgmental actions? Hardly! And it will look very different to the people around us than what they have rejected as "institutional religion" that has no place in their lives.

Here is my list of a few preliminary contrasts between the Institutional Church we seem to know best and the church many are beginning to envision and live out. The gap must be bridged sooner rather than later.

Institutional Church	Relational Church
Church is about getting our needs met through persons and programs	Church is about relating to God and others in authentic unselfishness
Scripture is a law book that is to be studied for its rules and formulas	Scripture is the narrative of God's patient and redemptive love for humans
Salvation is helping people get ready to go to heaven when they die	Salvation is divine rescue from an empty, vain, wasted life right now
Salvation is about people doing the right things	Salvation is the unmerited gift of God's grace
Stresses the distinction between being "in" and "out"	Sees us as pilgrims in search of God and is far less inclined to be judgmental
Known for being exclusive	Known for being inclusive
Emphasizes being right	Confesses its inadequacy
Being a "faithful church" requires avoiding people who are in error	We "grow together" to accept, hold accountable, and purify one another

Institutional Church	Relational Church
Church exists for "people like us" and makes others feel uncomfortable	Church is for reconciling diverse people and groups
Often heard: "Church must pay more attention to my needs!"	Often heard: "Church is a community where we learn to be unselfish"
Challenges insiders to help frame the institution's life and function for the benefit of the few	Functions as a loving community willing to support and nurture all who seek God with sincere hearts
External symbols and coded vocabulary are very important to identity	External symbols and coded vocabulary are avoided whenever possible
Worship is a defined, limited series of actions—sometimes marked off by a closing prayer before secular things	Worship is a way of life that envisions all its activities under God's will—with all things made sacred by the Spirit
"Missions" is the church's task of taking the gospel to foreign cultures	"Missions" is infiltration of the church's neighboring community

The idea of abandoning one way of "doing church" for a better approach to "being church" isn't really novel. Jesus described and caricatured the "Church of Religiosity" and the "Church of Love for God and Neighbor" for his time with the Parable of the Pharisee and the Tax Collector.

In my lower moments, I sometimes think Nietzsche was right! We keep turning the gold of faith into the lead of religion. We kill God anew in every generation and bury him in our church buildings. How is it that what Jesus promised to build, died to make possible, and rose to reign over from the Father's right hand came to so ignoble an end? What I do know is that the Received Church of my experience will not bring the people of our new world to God—but it will continue to drive them away from him.

Then I get a glimpse of God at work in an honest, struggling young man who fights through a terrible accident and horrible burns to gain a vibrant faith. I am blessed to visit, pray with, and encourage a woman who dies gracefully, though in agonizing pain from bone cancer. I take the word of their son's death to a couple whose response is to trust and praise God still, though through the bitterest of tears. Then I know I am wrong to be discouraged. It is the struggle of *every* generation to become aware that this challenge is what Father God knew we would experience, that his Living Spirit will continue to ensure that the "gates of Hades" will not prevail against the church, and that the Reigning Son will come again to claim his own. Kingdom Church has always been the unrealized goal of God among his people, and it will never be realized fully until he appears. In the meanwhile, we pray, dream, and refuse to be satisfied with "business as usual" for the Body of Christ.

There is more for us to experience in Christ than we can know in the Church of Sanctified Religiosity. And I am beginning to suspect that what we can only dream about and describe as Relational Church, the Church of Love for God and Neighbor, or Kingdom Church is really the old, original church that Christ promised to build and pledged to bless long ago. Maybe we have just been distracted for these 1700 years or so and are beginning to think more clearly and follow him more intentionally in view of Institutional Church's pronounced and all-too-public failures.

Chapter Three

"If You Love God, Burn the Church!"

"If there is a God, atheism must seem to Him as less of an insult than religion."
—Edmond de Goncourt

I once read a quote from some cynic who offered this advice: "If you love God, burn the church!" When I bumped into those words, the two episodes in Christ's life when he wreaked havoc in Herod's temple came to mind. And it is my conviction that this quote from our own time and those episodes from Jesus' career force us to face the unpleasant fact that it is easier for the church of this generation to take comfort in its nickels, numbers, and nails than it is to hear or to be a prophetic voice and presence in the world.

Spiritual renewal is an ongoing, never-finished work, but the tendency of a church —whether we are using the word to refer to a local congregation or an entire denomination or the so-called "church universal"—is to consolidate its gains, make peace with the status quo, and take care not to offend either its own or its neighbors.

It is time some of us got acquainted with the Jesus of Scripture who not only loved children and told charming stories but also became enraged when he saw spirituality reduced to trite religious rituals, human interpretations of Scripture used to hurt people, and religious leaders who used their authority to intimidate people into boring external conformity. This was Jesus before he was Christianized and turned into the brand name for a new religion. This was the unpredictable, brash prophet who later was tamed by the clergy and transformed into a disciplined, obliging shopkeeper.

Jesus at the Jerusalem Temple

The temple Jesus visited and where he participated in Jewish worship events is generally called "Herod's Temple" or "the Second Temple." Interestingly for Bible students, that fact provides one of the key chronological markers for studying the four Gospels and the life of Jesus. From Josephus, we know that Herod the Great began his project of refurbishing the temple in Jerusalem as an effort to win the political loyalty of the Jews around 19 BC.[1] So here—in the spring of AD 27—Jesus does something quite remarkable. He registers a not-so-subtle protest against what religion had done to the divine intention for a holy place and the spiritual exercises to be conducted there.

> The Passover of the Jews was near, and Jesus went up to Jerusalem. In the temple he found people selling cattle, sheep, and doves, and the money changers seated at their tables. Making a whip of cords, he drove all of them out of the temple, both the sheep and the cattle. He also poured out the coins of the money changers and overturned their tables. He told those who were selling the doves, "Take these things out of here! Stop making my Father's house a marketplace!" His disciples remembered that it was written, "Zeal for your house will consume me." The Jews then said to him, "What sign can you show us for doing this?" Jesus answered them, "Destroy this temple, and in three days I will raise it up." The Jews then said, "This temple has been under construction for forty-six years, and will you raise it up in three days?" But he

> was speaking of the temple of his body. After he was raised from the dead, his disciples remembered that he had said this; and they believed the scripture and the word that Jesus had spoken.
>
> When he was in Jerusalem during the Passover festival, many believed in his name because they saw the signs that he was doing. But Jesus on his part would not entrust himself to them, because he knew all people and needed no one to testify about anyone; for he himself knew what was in everyone. (John 2:13–25)

What an incredible thing for an aspiring young rabbi to do! One would expect him to court the religious power brokers, seek their blessing (funding?) for his proposed ministry, and be afraid of alienating them. But those expectations are probably colored significantly by what we would expect to happen in our own time and place.

The huge temple complex that covered about thirty-five acres in its heyday was under the control of the Jewish priesthood. That put them in charge of the temple's profitable business of providing animals that had passed inspection as suitable for sacrifice. It also meant that they ran the business of currency exchange that allowed adult Jewish males to pay the annual half-shekel tax to the temple treasury. That knowledge alone allows one to understand the comment from Jesus about the holy temple having been made into a marketplace or common bazaar.

These religious leaders were indignant over what Jesus had dared to do and called him to account for his actions. "What sign can you show us for doing this?" they demanded (John 2:18). Jesus replied with an enigmatic prediction of his death and resurrection, and that statement became clear to John and others only after the crucifixion (2:19–22).

It seems clear in retrospect that the events of that day constituted a "sign" about Jesus' view of the Religious Establishment (i.e., clergy, rituals, and trappings of *authorized* and *orthodox* religious practice). What he did was significant on a grand scale to align him with Old Testament prophets such as Amos and Isaiah. Nothing is worse than spiritual fervor that has lost its way. Nothing is more perverse than religion that serves to consolidate power and money for human leaders in the name of honoring God. Indeed, honest atheism is surely less of an insult to God than perverse and unethical behaviors in his name.

Although there is more to this episode of cleansing the temple, its most obvious and fundamental meaning is that God is terribly displeased when the forms of religious devotion are made into ends rather than means. Put another way, it is an offense to holiness when the worship and service of God is reduced to something that looks more like a business being run by the best practices of Harvard Business School than a spiritual exercise. Whether Jews of the first century or Christians of the twenty-first century, it is possible for our buildings, organizational structures, and rituals to get in the way of God's presence with us.

Jesus Then and Now

Do you ever get the feeling that we may have missed the point of what Jesus started out to do with the church? Maybe we should get off the backs of the priests and Levites or money changers and animal keepers at the temple two millennia ago and look at ourselves. Perhaps we should not feel quite so self-righteous in criticizing first-century Judaism but instead engage in a bit of introspection with contemporary Christianity.

Do you really think we have captured the essence of what Jesus died to make possible in what we now call Christendom? Do you really think we have it figured out so well in any one of our splintered denominations that its mission now is to sit in judgment on all the other "brands" of church? Is anybody arrogant enough to think that her or his congregation of pitiful sinners ought to be the measure for all other local churches? Oh, please!

Humility should be the easiest and most natural of the Christian virtues for those of us who pause to reflect on how far we are from the experience of the Christ one witnesses in the Gospels. In fact, humility seems to be among the last, hardest, and rarest of virtues for us.

If we had gotten the point of what was "signed" to us by the cleansing of the temple in Jerusalem, we never would have thought that what happens between 10 a.m. and noon on Sunday is the essence of our faith and sacred—while the rest of life is secular. If we'd gotten the point of those events from the personal experiences of God in the flesh, we'd never have come up with the idea that the money we put in the collection plate is God's—and the rest is ours for selfish purposes. If we had glimpsed even faintly what he was showing us on that raucous day when he railed against a worship-center-become-bazaar, we would never have fragmented the body of Christ with "worship wars" and power plays in Jesus' name—or a dozen other issues from Christian history that come to mind all too quickly. And I haven't even begun to list the weightier issues, such as the church's neglect of the poor, people in prison, sick persons, abused women, or unwanted children.

Christians have somehow come to be observers and consumers of religion rather than sold-out and surrendered imitators of Jesus of Nazareth. Churches have so reduced faith to times and places, ceremonies and traditions that the mere alteration of the time for those events or the order of the practices fosters panic. To say the least, I have received much more caustic complaints from church members over a half-hour change in service times than over ethnic groups without the Gospels in their own language or people being homeless in our city.

People with their spiritual priorities so obviously inverted have been led to believe that their church habits are equivalent to living a Christ-honoring, Christ-imitating lifestyle. Faith is ultimately much more than historical and philosophical grounding for one's worldview. It is the mystery of life-transformation by the power of the Holy Spirit at work in human personality. In the world of postmodernity, the best argument for the Christian faith is not a book or lecture but authentic discipleship among those who confess Christ.

Altering the church from an *organism* (i.e., the body of Christ that seeks the kingdom of God) into an *institution* (i.e., an organization that functions by the rules of the world) has had such unfortunate outcomes as these:

- Being a disciple-apprentice to Jesus of Nazareth was distorted from a Spirit-regenerated and Spirit-empowered lifestyle to simple church membership.
- Fellowship was perverted from loving involvement with a community of believers into group membership (i.e., "She is part of our fellowship") or church potlucks (i.e., "We'll be hosting a fellowship next Thursday at 6 p.m.").
- Worship ceased being an encounter with God and became morning or evening church assemblies.
- Evangelism stopped being a passionate connection with and loving confrontation of the world with the gospel and became inviting people to hear a visitor preach for the weekend or giving them sixteen-page pamphlets.
- Communion was somehow robbed of its identity as an interactive meal and turned into a funereal ceremony to be observed in silence.
- Discipleship ceased being self-denial, struggle, and growth and became training seminars every other year.
- Leadership was modified from Spirit-empowered passion and gifts that served people to a flowchart of titles and offices.
- Bible study degenerated from challenging and life-transforming obedience into listening sessions.
- Popular conceptions of the hallmarks of Christian faith ceased to be righteousness, peace, and joy in the Holy Spirit and came to be meanness, guilt, and fear.

Can we honestly think it was only Judaism that degenerated over time into customs, practices, and outcomes far removed from God's original purpose? Has the same thing not happened in our own Christian history?

Would Jesus Join Your Church?

What do you think would happen if Jesus showed up in Rome, London, New York, or Los Angeles today? Which church would he join? Or would his eyes flash with anger? Might he just disavow *all* of us? Would he drive some preachers out of their pulpits? Or would he be pleased with how attentive we are to one another and how well we take care of each other? Would he be impressed by our passion for representing him faithfully to the world both in terms of compassion and holiness?

We need a prophetic presence and voice in our midst. But I wonder if we would tolerate Jesus any better now than we did originally. We just might kill him again.

When Alice stumbled into Wonderland, she was disoriented by the fantastic characters she met and strange experiences she had. But the world she encountered there pales by comparison to the upside-down world we encounter in the kingdom of God. Deity became human, King became peasant, and Creator God became Suffering Servant. When he could not hide his true identity any longer, he still claimed no special privileges —living a selfless, obedient life and dying a selfless, obedient death. God the Son lived in humility and submission to God the Father. Now he has been exalted and proclaimed Lord of All—in the good timing of the Father. Our challenge as his apprentices is to follow his example.

"Do nothing out of selfish ambition or vain conceit, but in humility consider others better than yourselves," wrote Paul. "Each of you should look not only to your own interests, but also to the interests of others. Your attitude should be the same as that of Christ Jesus" (Phil. 2:3–5 NIV). Or, in *The Message*, "Don't push your way to the front; don't sweet-talk your way to the top. Put yourself aside, and help others get ahead. Don't be obsessed with getting your own advantage. Forget yourselves long enough to lend a helping hand. Think of yourselves the way Christ Jesus thought of himself."

Sinful human nature cries out for the right of self-rule. The life goals that spring from the I've-gotta-be-me creed are always selfish and frequently result in others being manipulated, used, hurt, and cast aside. For someone with that mindset to consider what it would mean to live under God's rule is abhorrent.

Life apart from heaven's reign in our lives is focused on getting and using things for personal advancement—money, power, education, sex, name recognition, awards, *whatever*. You name it. Leadership is conceived on the model of giving orders and enforcing compliance—in a home, at work, with a church. If others have to be coerced or stepped on, so much the worse for them. And "winning" is the obsession that drives every decision and every relationship. *It's all about me!*

One who does not live under the kingdom reign of God—even if he or she is a good church member—must have the last word. Push others around. Strut in victory. Pout in defeat. She is seldom honest with others and never with herself. He cries for himself but not for others. She wants to be heard but cannot listen. He is angry and finds fault with practically everything and everybody. She forgives nothing and remembers every slight—whether real or imagined—that ever came her way. *It* is *all about me!*

When Christians petition God and pray, "Your kingdom come, your will be done on earth as it is in heaven," we are asking God to help us get over ourselves. We are pleading to have the attitude of Christ Jesus that allowed him to be humble, selfless, deferential, obedient—and to leave vindication and honor to God the Father, in his own good time. Love and peace, kindness and gentleness, patience and joy, humility and goodness, self-control and righteousness—these are the Spirit-generated features of a world so different from the ordinary that it looks upside down to everybody who sees it. These characteristics are more bizarre and unreal than anything Lewis Carroll pictured in *Alice in Wonderland*. But they are not illusions. They are the ultimate realities of the kingdom of God.

One day, Jesus watched the sort of jockeying for attention and position that is so common among human beings. He had been invited to a Sabbath meal at the house of a top Jewish figure in a Galilean town he was visiting. Here is what he saw and said:

> When he noticed how the guests picked the places of honor at the table, he told them this parable: "When someone invites you to a wedding feast, do not take the place of honor, for a person more distinguished than you may have been invited. If so, the host who invited both of you will come and say to you, 'Give this man your seat.' Then, humiliated, you will have to take the least important place. But when you are invited, take the lowest place, so that when your host comes, he will say to you, 'Friend, move up to a better place.' Then you will be honored in the presence of all your fellow guests. For everyone who exalts himself will be humbled, and he who humbles himself will be exalted." (Luke 14:7–11 NIV)

Pride, status, and recognition are issues in every culture—and the one within which Jesus moved was no exception. He watched as guests arriving for dinner moved around a U-shaped dining table. Since the positions of greatest honor were naturally the ones closest to the host's chair, everyone was elbowing toward those special seats. So he imagines an even bigger social event with an even larger table and the sort of seat-jockeying that situation would generate. Then he pictures the humiliation someone would suffer when, after getting a choice seat, his host "demotes" him when a really significant guest shows up. Why, the only seats left by that time would be the ones at the greatest distance from the host. What utter humiliation for the seat-jockey; what regard for the late-arriving but genuinely important person who gets his seat.

Jesus' point here is hardly that his disciples should be conniving. Go late to get noticed. Or take a lowlier seat than you know your host is going to grant in order to be called to a better one. To the contrary, he is trying to make us see that honor in the kingdom of God is not for the taking. It is God's to award by grace. So it is out of character for his followers to worry about or jockey for it. "For everyone who exalts himself will be humbled, and he who humbles himself will be exalted" is another way of saying that the way up for you is down, or that the surest way for me to crowd God out is by being too full of myself.

The Gospel of Luke has a theme many scholars have noted and to which they have called attention. It is called "eschatological reversal"—when the end comes, things will be very different than they are now; high things will be brought low, and lowly things will be honored; rich and proud people will be in spiritual poverty, while the humble poor will be given honor and wealth and status. The disciple who cannot imitate Christ's selfless obedience will miss out on the joy of his exaltation to the Father's right hand.

The Challenge: "Grow Up!"

One of the shortest Psalms is attributed to David and appeals for Israel to have unwavering faith in Yahweh. It anticipates this teaching from Jesus: "I tell you the truth, unless you change and become like little children, you will never enter the kingdom of heaven. Therefore, whoever humbles himself like this child is the greatest in the kingdom of heaven" (Matt. 18:3–4 NIV).

> My heart is not proud, O Lord,
> my eyes are not haughty;
> I do not concern myself with great matters

> or things too wonderful for me.
> But I have stilled and quieted my soul;
> like a weaned child with its mother,
> like a weaned child is my soul within me.
>
> O Israel, put your hope in the Lord
> both now and forevermore. (Ps. 131:1–3 NIV)

This psalm goes against everything modernity has trumpeted for more than two centuries now. We do not have to accept things as they are; we are the masters of our own destinies. We do not have to suffer or cry or wait; we are entitled to the things we want, and we are entitled to them now. We do not have to submit ourselves to God and trust him amidst life's uncertainties; we are autonomous people who can trust only ourselves.

Walter Brueggemann comments on Psalm 131 and writes:

> The piety reflected in this psalm is directly opposed to modernity with its drive toward independence, self-sufficiency, and autonomy. It is worth noting that the Psalms deny the Oedipal inclination that there can be freedom only if the controlling, authoritarian father-god be slain or denied. The myth of modernity believes that real maturity is to be free of every relationship of dependence. But when the metaphor is changed from a harsh controlling father to a gently feeding mother, it is evident that the human goal need not be breaking away, but happy trust.[2]

What strikes me from this psalm is the figure of a weaned child as opposed to a still-nursing infant. Looking ahead again to the New Testament, being a Christian begins with being "born from above" (John 3:1–5), proceeds through a gradual process of growth toward maturity (Heb. 6:1–3), and moves toward an adult state of faith and life (James 1:4). And it is interesting that both Hebrews and James—epistles that deal with the desirability of growth toward maturity—do so in the context of teaching believers how to respond to hardship and suffering.

So the unnamed writer of Hebrews counsels us to "endure hardship as discipline" (12:7), and the brother of Jesus says that trials test our faith in order to teach us perseverance (1:2-4). Hardship and trials are for the sake of testing, refinement, and maturity; they are not allowed in human experience to destroy us—though Satan would like to see them produce that outcome. If we react to them in authentic submission to and trust in God, however, they become the means to growth. They make us stronger. They mature us into the very image of God's perfect Son who learned obedience through the things he suffered (Heb. 5:8–9).

Too many of us seem never to get beyond the nursing baby who is totally self-absorbed and self-centered. Now, mothers, don't get me wrong here! There's nothing wrong with a tiny baby being what tiny babies are. But you are not going to want your cute, demanding, squalling-whenever-hungry baby to be that way at three or nine or sixteen. And it is part of your responsibility as a good mother to bring your baby girl to the point that she can—while not renouncing you or failing to understand your importance during the move from infancy through adolescence to adulthood—learn that the world does not revolve around her.

In other words, part of your job as a parent is to teach your baby not to be a baby forever. It involves you helping him understand that your role in life is not to spoil him but to train him for life in the real world. The weaning process for an infant can be excruciatingly difficult. A baby is suddenly denied the right to on-demand feeding, on-demand comfort, on-demand meeting of his needs. And it is no easier a few years later when it is the cutting of apron strings for an adolescent or the shutting down of cash flow for the young adult. But these are all stages in growing up.

Isn't it possible that some of us are insisting on the right to perpetual infancy in our faith lives? Why do we complain so bitterly when life disappoints us? Why is it "unfair" that we suffer? Why is God suddenly unworthy of worship when I am denied the instant gratification of a nursing baby and expected to learn that the world can be hostile? That it's not all about me? Psalm 131 says that we will not be allowed the immature state of being spoiled brats in God's house.

A weaned child is no less dependent on his mother than a nursing one; for God's children, the weaning process is designed to move us away from immature self-centeredness to trust. Just as an infant must learn that his mother does not exist only to satisfy his desires and that he should love her for her own sake, so must the people of God grow up enough that we love God for his own sake and not simply because he's a wish-granter in our self-centered universe.

So what is humility? What does it mean to "get over ourselves"? For one thing, it is to realize the true nature of human life. The universe doesn't revolve around me, and God doesn't exist to pull rabbits out of a hat for you, either. For another, as we experience the harsh realities of light and darkness, good and evil, we live with the sure confidence that God is not far from us. He is sovereign and will not let us be destroyed by anything below, for he has higher, eternal plans for us. Finally, we experience God not just in the moments of joy and contentment but in the times of great stress and intense struggle. We walk by faith and look to the example of Jesus as one who endured with an eye to the goal. Honoring God. Trusting his grace. Knowing that he does not forget his promises.

Churches Can Get in God's Way

I have been in Jerusalem only once. It was wonderful to visit the temple mount and to know I was looking at some of the very foundation stones of that compound Jesus and Paul would have seen. I strained to hear the anguished pleas of my Lord in Gethsemane. And I was overwhelmed with emotion as I traced the steps of the Son of Man from Pilate's Judgment Hall along the Via Dolorosa to Golgotha.

At each of the critical sites, however, there was a distracting—and sometimes even disgusting—problem. Each one of them had a church or shrine built over it that obscured what I had come to see. Then it dawned on me: *Churches are bad about getting in the way of people who simply want to see Jesus.* We too often obscure rather than illuminate his presence by our divisions, our hypocrisies, and our sinfulness.

What Jesus did in cleansing the temple is good background for understanding what he told a Samaritan woman beside Jacob's well. Jerusalem or Gerazim, Rome or London, Nairobi or Detroit—the site for worship is irrelevant. Since Jesus has been raised from the dead, the only issue of critical relevance is no longer where but whom to worship. As he said so enigmatically in John 2, the real temple for his followers is his own body—torn down and then rebuilt in just three days. Every knee must bow and every tongue must confess that Jesus Christ is Lord. All who worship the Father in Spirit and in Truth will receive heaven's blessing.

Let's hope we won't have to "burn the church" to prove our love for God. Let's hope "Christendom" won't have to be made illegal by some anti-Christian conqueror to make some of us discover the centrality of Christ. But we will have to continue the perpetual questioning and reform of our religious categories. We will have to be vigilant about living relational rather than institutional faith. And we must be very careful not to cut ourselves off from the One whose name we wear by so recasting him in our fallen image that we cannot be transformed into his glorious likeness.

Chapter Four

Religion as "Gamesmanship"

"My faith in Christ is central to my life. . . . But following Christ does not mean following his followers."
—Anne Rice

Announcing on her Facebook page that she was doing it "in the name of Christ," author Anne Rice told her fans on July 28, 2010, that she was giving up Christianity.

If you are a Christian, take offense at her public remark, and are prepared to write her off as either someone who must not have been a believer in the first place or just another angry celebrity denouncing Jesus, hold on for a moment. If, on the other hand, you are not a Christian and expect henceforth to count Ms. Rice a statistical ally as a non-Christian or atheist, that judgment too needs to be held in abeyance. Even more, for anyone who is hostile toward Jesus or ready to attack the core tenets of the Christian faith, it would be premature to expect aid and comfort.

Ms. Rice's statement is in some ways unremarkable. As a Christian theologian, I am in sympathy with it. As someone who has spent his adult life in church ministry, I have heard many others say the same thing. Several things about her life and career combine, however, to generate discussion that could be very helpful to many people.

Anne Rice has sold over seventy-five million books. Best known for *Interview with the Vampire* and other gothic novels, she had renounced the Roman Catholic religion of her youth at age eighteen. As an adult, she not only became a successful writer but also sought to understand her son's life as a gay man, lost her five-year-old granddaughter to leukemia, and (along with her late husband) struggled with alcoholism.

Following surgery and a diabetic coma that almost took her life, she renewed her commitment to the Catholic faith in 1998.

Since that recommitment and its public documentation in 2008 with *Called Out of Darkness: A Spiritual Confession*, she has dedicated herself to "glorifying God" and launched a series of *Christ the Lord* books. The first of them, *Out of Egypt*, is the fictionalized account of a seven-year-old Jesus leaving Egypt with his family for Nazareth. So what *does* her "quitting Christianity" statement mean? Has she decided now that God doesn't exist after all? Jesus was a fraud? The Bible is a myth? Hardly.

Christ and the Games Played in His Name

In her initial posting, Anne Rice said she refused to be anti-gay, anti-feminist, anti-science, anti-artificial birth control, anti-Democrat. Here is the crux: "For those who care, and I understand if you don't: Today I quit being a Christian. I'm out. I remain committed to Christ as always but not to being 'Christian' or part of Christianity. It's simply impossible for me to 'belong' to this quarrelsome, hostile, disputatious, and deservedly infamous group. For ten years, I've tried. I've failed. I'm an outsider. My conscience will allow nothing else."

She followed up the next day with this: "My faith in Christ is central to my life. My conversion from a pessimistic atheist lost in a world I don't understand, to an optimistic believer in a universe created and sustained by a loving God is crucial to me. But following Christ does not mean following His followers."

The sixty-eight-year-old writer is neither despairing of nor denouncing Jesus Christ. She is articulating her despair over hateful attitudes, unreasoning postures, mean-spirited behaviors, and un-Jesus-like actions across history—and in the present time—by people who have invoked his name over evils ranging from anti-Semitism to child abuse, from Klan cross-burnings to televangelist sex-and-money scandals. Indeed, she is echoing the line of theologian Karl Barth: "Religion is the great enemy of God." Indeed, more evil has been perpetrated in the name of religion than by any other institutional power across the centuries of human history.

Ms. Rice has not been guilty of blasphemy. She has stated the obvious and joined the ranks of Isaiah, Amos, John the Baptist, Jesus, James, John, and Paul to say that authentic faith must be purged of ignorance, hatred, denial, and hypocrisy. She could have cited these lines from the Hebrew Bible: "I want no more pious meetings. . . . Your festivals are a burden to me. . . . When you lift your hands to pray, I will not listen. . . . Seek justice. Help the oppressed. Defend the cause of orphans. Fight for the rights of widows" (Isa. 1:13–17 NLT). Or she might have quoted this from one of the latest sections of the New Testament: "There are people who act 'religious'—all the while rejecting the power that would make them truly godly. Stay away from people like that!" (2 Tim. 3:5 NLT).

Neither these biblical writers nor Ms. Rice used the language of "life-changing personal faith" over against "institutional religion." All their statements translate easily into such a distinction. One is no more a Christian by virtue of being a church member than one is a physician by entering a hospital or a corpse by going to a funeral home. The simplistic tendency is to equate church membership, religious ritual, Christianity, Catholicism, Protestantism, or nondenominationalism with being *a follower of Jesus Christ*, but they may be light years apart from each other. To be clear, they are certainly compatible but not always synonymous.

While some Rwandan churches and Christians acted nobly during the genocidal events of 1994, the much-touted triumph of "Christianity" in that African nation did not prevent the catastrophe. The best evidence is that ethnic hatred was preached and ethnic violence perpetrated by priests, evangelists, deacons, pastors, and members across all denominational lines. Rwanda was well populated with Christian church buildings, Christian schools, Christian ministries, Christian *whatevers*—but it was woefully deficient in terms of love for God that could be witnessed in love for one's neighbors.

While some American churches and Christians model virtue and "do what is right, love mercy, and walk humbly with God," others have been known to fly the banner of "Christianity" over judgmentalism, gay-bashing, the love of money and power, racist hatred, and insensitivity to the weak and powerless whom Jesus served.

Some might say, "But Christians are obligated to 'take a stand' against secular humanists, sexual perverts, and drunkards!" Yes. Of course. But the purest example of taking issues and people to task comes from Jesus. He treated people with respect. He ate with them. He defended them from religious zealots ready to stone them. In fact, the Gospels show Jesus to be "in their face" and using the language of strong censure against religious zealots. Those enthusiasts for certain Old Testament rules have their counterparts in the fire-breathing devotees of selected New Testament teachings today.

First-century Judaism had its rigid moralists who were willing to stone an adulterous woman rather than give mercy a chance. Twenty-first-century Islam has its radical adherents who clamor to impose *Sharia* on secular societies. We close our eyes to the obvious when we deny that Christianity has its own vocal-and-intolerant element that is willing to shoot first and get the facts later. Thus we have not a single famous author rejecting practitioners of *that* brand of pseudo-Christianity, but countless others who have either been wounded personally or been filled with righteous indignation at the sight of such Christians' acrimony and malicious treatment of people who need help.

Despite denunciations that immediately began to come her way, Anne Rice merely dared to speak a prophetic truth about religious system-building over against simple faith in Jesus of Nazareth, or groupthink versus conscience. I hear her deploring judgment and appealing for grace. I hear her saying that she could no longer play games in the name of the religion she had re-embraced a few years ago.

Many of us have rescued personal faith from dogmatic shackles by distinguishing between following Jesus and swallowing whole what others have offered in his name. Others, sadly, have simply walked away—tossing out the baby with the bathwater, throwing away the redemptive Christ with a repressive experience of something that called itself Christianity.

Jesus and Religious Gamesmanship

There is a section in the Gospel of Mark that plops us down in the middle of a series of arguments forced on Jesus by his critics and enemies. A series of self-appointed guardians of orthodoxy came to Jesus in rapid succession, hoping to "expose" him with their trick questions. In the process, they revealed their hearts. They saw religion as gamesmanship. It was the playing field on which one person could win and another would have to lose. It was their means to expose, humiliate, and otherwise destroy someone with whom they disagreed. It was power—the power to admit or exclude, elevate or ridicule, honor or shame.

> Then they sent to him some Pharisees and some Herodians to trap him in what he said. And they came and said to him, "Teacher, we know that you are sincere, and show deference to no one; for you do not regard people with partiality, but teach the way of God in accordance with truth. Is it lawful to pay taxes to the emperor, or not? Should we pay them, or should we not?" But knowing their hypocrisy, he said to them, "Why are you putting me to the test? Bring me a denarius and let me see it." And

> they brought one. Then he said to them, "Whose head is this, and whose title?" They answered, "The emperor's." Jesus said to them, "Give to the emperor the things that are the emperor's, and to God the things that are God's." And they were utterly amazed at him.
>
> Some Sadducees, who say there is no resurrection, came to him and asked him a question, saying, "Teacher, Moses wrote for us that if a man's brother dies, leaving a wife but no child, the man shall marry the widow and raise up children for his brother. There were seven brothers; the first married and, when he died, left no children; and the second married her and died, leaving no children; and the third likewise; none of the seven left children. Last of all the woman herself died. In the resurrection whose wife will she be? For the seven had married her."
>
> Jesus said to them, "Is not this the reason you are wrong, that you know neither the scriptures nor the power of God? For when they rise from the dead, they neither marry nor are given in marriage, but are like angels in heaven. And as for the dead being raised, have you not read in the book of Moses, in the story about the bush, how God said to him, 'I am the God of Abraham, the God of Isaac, and the God of Jacob'? He is God not of the dead, but of the living; you are quite wrong." (Mark 12:13–27)

Jesus got caught up in their games because he couldn't avoid it. They made him their target, so he could not avoid them altogether. But he didn't make a career of this nonsense! He had spent the bulk of his time to this point in his ministry teaching, preparing, and empowering his own disciples—and avoiding the religious authorities. But things were moving to an end quickly now. He had come to Jerusalem. The shadow of the cross was falling over him. He walked into the "trap" of his enemies because there was no longer any reason to avoid it.

It all started with his challenge to what went on habitually at the temple. He went through the Court of the Gentiles and turned the noisy bazaar into stunned amazement. "You have made [my father's house] into a den of thieves!" he roared. Thus began a series of five confrontations: (1) a demand to know the "authority" by which Jesus had cleansed the temple at 11:27–33; (2) the very pointed Parable of the Owner's Son at 12:1–12; (3) the challenge about paying Roman taxes at 12:13–17; (4) a trick question about married life in the post-resurrection world at 12:18–27; and (5) an inquiry about the "greatest commandment" in Torah at 12:28–34.

For our purposes right now, suffice it to say that these confrontations accomplished two things. First, they demonstrated the absolute brilliance of Jesus. He didn't get tripped up by his enemies. To the contrary, he effectively silenced them. They stopped trying to goad him with their trap-setting questions because the confrontations were backfiring on them; they decided instead simply to resort to brute force to get rid of him. Thus, second, these confrontations sealed Jesus' fate.

Rather than walk through all these questions and answers in detail, I'd like to step back and raise awareness of the larger issues surrounding them. And I want to use the larger lesson from this text to caution us against allowing religion to be nothing more than gamesmanship in our own experience. Or, to echo the language of Alcoholics Anonymous again, I want to caution all of us against substituting the husks of religion for the nourishment of authentic spirituality.

Maybe it would help to make the lessons of this text more personal by telling you the true stories of two people I have known. Their stories are both matters of public record, so I am not breaking any confidences. Even so, I will disguise the main characters by altering a few of their details for the sake of keeping identities concealed. That is, the names will be changed to protect the not-so-innocent people involved. But the skeleton of each story is absolutely (and frighteningly!) true. I hope their stories are uncharacteristic of Christ-confessing people.

True Stories of Two People

The first is the story of a preacher. I had met him a few times over the years, but I could not say that we knew each other well enough to be friends. He had preached for a very conservative church, in fact, and I heard that he had taken a few shots at me and at the church I was serving at the time. Big deal! People sometimes criticize other people because they either don't have all the facts or don't know the motives behind certain things others do. At other times, they criticize because the people involved deserve criticism. If I wrote off everybody who doesn't like something I've done or said, I'd have to leave the planet.

That preacher was fired from the church where he had worked for more than ten years when it was discovered that he had sexually abused three children in his church—his own eleven-year-old daughter and two of her friends. He and his wife separated, and he moved to the city where I was living in order to search for a job. A friend of mine from a church nearby called to tell me what had happened. My sense was that he thought I might take some satisfaction in the report. I didn't—and told him so.

People sometimes go over the edge when they do something as terrible as that preacher had done. They figure they have nothing to lose and throw away what is left of their lives. Some are so overwhelmed with shame that they commit suicide. So I set about to track him down, invite him to lunch, and offer to be of whatever help I could to him. I wanted him to know that God's redemptive power was for him—not just for those to whom he had once preached. He agreed to meet me at a restaurant.

We arrived within a couple of minutes of each other. We stood in the foyer making small talk while waiting for a table. Then, when a hostess seated us, I prayed again for God to give me the right opening and correct words to let him know that I cared about him and wanted to help him get things back on track in his life. But he took the initiative in our conversation. "There are some doctrines I've heard you believe that I need to let you know I disagree with," he started. It didn't make me angry. It made me sad. A poor fellow with a log in his eye felt the need to pick sawdust out of mine.

The second story is that of a college student. She grew up in a Christian home. Both the folks back home and those of us who had gotten to know her in the city where she was attending college thought highly of her. She is bright and outgoing. She has friends galore. But some things had been going wrong in her life, and she trusted me enough to ask for an appointment to talk with me.

She had been experimenting with alcohol and marijuana for over a year, and she had done cocaine once recently. She said she really didn't see as much danger in any of that as her parents did—or as she presumed I might. Her immediate concern was that she had found out three days before that she had gonorrhea. She had slept with three different guys a number of times during the past year. "But I haven't missed church one time since leaving home for college," she told me. "Even when one of those guys and I would spend the weekend together out of town, I'd make him get up and go to church with me on Sunday morning."

What's Wrong with These Pictures?

What's wrong with these two stories? Does anything about either of them grate at you? Does anything strike you as inappropriate?

Both these true stories reflect real-life instances of church members who just don't get it. They know how to "do church" but don't know how to live in holiness and compassion. One was living a tradition-bound faith that could somehow tolerate child molestation for over three years but could not abide something he regarded as a doctrinal error related to the ongoing worship wars in our churches. The other was living her parents' faith about the importance of attending church services, while her own lifestyle contradicted some basic values those assemblies surely affirmed.

The late Paul Little used to distinguish three kinds of faith. The first two can be, in his words, "strictly environmental, an outgrowth of your surroundings."

Some people have *indoctrination faith*. They have gone to the right places, have sung the right hymns, and can give all the right answers about what they call the plan of salvation. They wouldn't think of missing church without a really good reason. They can quote a lot of Bible verses. But they have never really met the Christ they have studied about, and they have no life-changing personal commitment to him.

Then there are people with *conformity faith*. These people do reasonably well when they are in Christian surroundings. When they are in a church assembly, in a school or work environment surrounded by Christians, or with their families, they do all the right things and practically none of the wrong ones. Put them with people whose values and behavior are sub-Christian or leave them to make their own decisions about what to do, however, and—to use Little's words—they will "shed their faith like a raincoat."

The third kind of faith is called *commitment faith*. This is the faith that goes deeper than tradition, family, or mere intellectual acceptance of the facts about Jesus. It is life-changing commitment to Jesus as Lord. It is serious obedience to the Word of God. It is a life of genuine discipleship that denies self, takes up one's cross, and follows Jesus.

The Alternative of Authenticity

Jesus lived among people who argued over paying taxes to a pagan government but thought nothing of plotting to kill him. No, that's not correct. They thought they were doing the right thing to rid the world of Jesus—by whatever wicked means necessary. Some of those same people spent hours every week fasting, praying, and studying Scripture—but they didn't know God. They were hair-splitters and synagogue-attenders, but they could have no part in the kingdom of God. They were happy to argue religion all day but would permit a widow to starve or let an orphan sleep in the streets. They had reduced religion to gamesmanship. They were members of the one true Church of Moses, could quote the Ten Commandments by heart, and wouldn't think of violating the Sabbath. But they were hopelessly lost.

As much as you love your parents, their faith cannot be transmitted to you like eye and hair color. As much as you love your children, you don't want them to have your faith but their own personal commitment to Christ. As much as you respect the church heritage in which you were reared, you need a faith grounded in a personal relationship with Jesus Christ rather than in a particular historical tradition. Otherwise, the gamesmanship of the Christian religion replaces the spiritual authenticity of a disciple of Jesus.

Chapter Five

THE MEDIUM REALLY *IS* THE MESSAGE

"After Constantine, blessedly bereft of powers of imposition, the church must indeed be the message it wishes a watchful world to hear and embrace."
—RODNEY CLAPP

> While Jesus was still talking to the crowd, his mother and brothers stood outside, wanting to speak to him. Someone told him, "Your mother and brothers are standing outside, wanting to speak to you." He replied to him, "Who is my mother, and who are my brothers?" Pointing to his disciples, he said, "Here are my mother and my brothers. For whoever does the will of my Father in heaven is my brother and sister and mother." (Matt. 12:46–50 NIV)

Was Jesus being disrespectful to his family in this scene? Was he getting back at his unbelieving and insulting brothers—all of whom made fun of his messianic claims until after the resurrection? Was he impolite to his own mother here? I think not. To the contrary, he was making the very significant point that relationships formed by faith are more important than our dearest natural ties. He was teaching that to be united with him in the pursuit of the kingdom of God is a closer alliance than any that can be created by flesh and blood. To use the language of a paraphrase that captures his point precisely, Jesus was saying, "Obedience is thicker than blood. The person who obeys my heavenly Father's will is my brother and sister and mother" (Matt. 12:50 MSG).

In this reaction to his closest relatives, Jesus was performing a truth he had already spoken. Earlier in the Gospel of Matthew, he told his followers that biological families would be divided on account of him. Do you recall what he said about brothers turning against siblings and parents and children being alienated on account of him (10:21–22)? "Anyone who loves his father or mother more than me is not worthy of me," he added. "Anyone who loves his son or daughter more than me is not worthy of me" (10:37). Strong language! Again, however, it is not meant to disparage what we have come to call the nuclear human family but to magnify the value of extended family in Christ. To affirm the solidarity of the faith community formed around him. To tell us just how important the concept of church as *Family of God* actually is.

So long as church is a place or a series of events on certain days and at certain times, it will continue to have minimal-to-decreasing influence for changing the world. It will continue to create unhealthy dependence by the many on the few and preserve our focus on externals as measurements of Christian life and maturity.

To the contrary, if we could rid ourselves of the debilitating effects of institutionalized religiosity—what has passed for "Christianity" over the past 1700 years—and enter the experience of God's life-giving presence in Christ, everything would change. As the authentic body of Christ in the world, such a church would turn the world upside down again. *The medium would become the message* of rescue and renewal.

Church would not be something to "do" but would be experienced as who Christ's followers are everywhere, with everybody, all the time. Worship would no longer be a place to "go" but would be the offering of our bodies as living sacrifices. Our outreach would not be a "program" but would be touching people with acceptance, love, and nurture that honors and imitates Jesus himself.

When Medium Becomes Message

I once sat in a crowded room in Jerusalem as a young Arab woman told about her journey to Christ. She told of some Christians she had known and of being introduced to the gospel. Then she told what happened to her when her (biological) family learned that she had befriended some Christ-followers and was learning the Jesus Story with sympathy and appreciation. Her father and brother beat her to within an inch of her life! They warned her that she would get the same thing again if she had further contact with those people. And they told her they would kill her if she should choose ever to be baptized.

Christians sometimes miss the point of baptism. For some it is sprinkling a little water on a baby's head to dedicate her to Christ or to signify that an adult has joined a particular denomination. Even those of us who practice full-body immersion can still miss the point by seeing baptism principally as a human decision to affiliate with either a particular denomination or a local church. But have you ever thought about these words from the prologue to the Gospel of John? "To all who received [Jesus], to those who believed in his name, he gave the right to become children of God—children born not of natural descent, nor of human decision or a husband's will, but born of God" (1:12–13 NIV).

The critical importance of baptism is not the "decision for Christ" it represents on the part of a believer but the act of God in giving new-birth life, from-above life to that person. Born of water and Spirit, the baptized man or woman has God as Father, Jesus as Redeemer from all that has gone before, and Holy Spirit as Indwelling Presence to empower the future. Baptism—when properly taught and understood—is not "human performance" but divine activity, not "our good work" but God's grace, not "our part in salvation" but heaven's sign to us. It is a sign of washing away sin—not in water but by blood. It is the sign of death, burial, and resurrection to new life—Christ's confessed and our own claimed. It is birth from above that is signified to us through the whole-body event of immersion in water—and made effective for whole-life transformation by quickening from the dead by the Holy Spirit.

Back now to that twenty-something Arab girl in Jerusalem. Her Islamic family knew more about the meaning of baptism than some Christians grasp. They understood that baptism in the name of Jesus would be for her to swap her Muslim past for a Christian future. They told her in no uncertain terms that if she embraced Christ, she would destroy forever her place in their family. We could only hope to have her courage in facing threats so stark and dangerous; they told her that her dabbling with Christianity had set her against her family and would result in more punishment—even punishment intended to kill her—if it did not come to an end immediately.

So there she stood in a church assembly where both Jewish and Arab believers were listening to her words. Through her tears, she told a hundred or so people that they would henceforth have to be her family. In her confession with words and in baptism, she was confirming the words of Jesus again: "Don't imagine that I came to bring peace to the earth! No, I came to bring a sword. I have come to set a man against his father, and a daughter against her mother, and a daughter-in-law against her mother-in-law. Your enemies will be right in your own household!" (Matt. 10:34–36 NLT).

When we have been born into the Family of God, we are committed to the first commandment of the Christian faith—to love God with our total being. We not only have God as our Father, however; we now have each other as extended family. And the same divine call and inclusion that made us children to God make us brothers and sisters to one another and challenge us to learn the second commandment of the Christian faith—to love each other as we love ourselves. We dare not simply rub shoulders with one another occasionally but must learn to treat each other as dear relatives in the Family of God.

You Just Can't Go It Alone

Paul Tournier once claimed there are two things one cannot do alone—be married and be a Christian. He is right. The essence of being a Christian is not an extended set of correct doctrinal beliefs or even well-formed personal character. To be a Christian is to be connected to Christ in such a unique and special way that all other relationships are defined by that union. The perfect triune fellowship of God as Father, Son, and Spirit from eternity past has been opened to me by the blood of Jesus at Calvary. But I cannot experience their fellowship in isolation from all others who have been called into it.

Institutional Church functions more as a restaurant than as a family to its members. Individuals or families or tiny clusters of friends come in. They find either a private, isolated booth in the corner or a table large enough for their little group. They sit and talk with one another—hardly aware that anybody else is present unless, of course, somebody gets their customary seats or blocks their line of sight. They order, eat, and exit. They'll be back when they get hungry again. Otherwise, they feel no real connection with the people who shared the room with them for an hour. And a new menu at the church down the street or an alteration of the familiar one at the old place may well create a new "loyalty" overnight. That is the language of franchise restaurants rather than family—and of Institutional Church rather than Relational Church.

When church is lived relationally and functions as family, however, a gathering is more like a family reunion than a restaurant visit. The family can respect its members so that introverts are not asked to behave as extroverts, but everybody senses a warm welcome and blessing. Having others around is not a nuisance but a necessity for families. These interactions shape us. We sing and read, stand and bow, laugh and cry. And, yes, we certainly eat and drink together. But we do all these things as a network of friends. We are a gathering of family members. We are a church whose identity is not contained in itself but is found in the God who has formed it.

This is the church of Acts 2 that had occasional big gatherings for worship and instruction. Those events could inspire them with accounts of what God was doing in their midst. They were in awe of God-presence moving among them (vs. 42-43)! All those people didn't know each other's names! That is why that same church had house-to-house gatherings for the cultivation of friendships, encouragement in faith, and accountability. These things combined to nurture their ever-deepening relationship with Christ as Lord.

The lordship of Christ played out within the internal relationships of the Jerusalem church not only in education and worship but in spiritual formation. They cared enough for one another that they would sell possessions and pool the proceeds to help one another (vs. 44–45). They were treating one another not as occasional restaurant guests who began to recognize each other's faces in public but as true family members. They seem to have had no concern whatever to jockey for church offices or perks. They cared about one another and showed their concern in very practical ways.

Their commitment to Jesus and to one another created the opportunity for that original church to tell the gospel message to others. And the church grew very naturally and organically—not by campaigns, crusades, and marketing strategies (vs. 47). Do you hear how *relational* all this sounds? How *personal*? How *communal*? How *familial*?

Acceptance, Accountability, and Nurture

A visitor entering a healthy church community senses that these people are dearest friends. They are extended family to one another. They are brothers and sisters in Christ. The stories that emerge from contact with those people are accounts of shared joys and sorrows, extended family helping nuclear families through crises of all sorts. Many of those stories are, in fact, prefaced with accounts of backgrounds in which churches had functioned more as schools giving occasional doctrinal exams or companies measuring productivity. So some tell of being kicked out (or being made to feel unwanted) because they didn't measure up to production-conversion quotas. Others tell of giving up in discouragement because they couldn't even talk without fear to their "leaders." They saw and disagreed with some of the pronouncements and judgments being made against others but realized their own doubts or disagreements or spiritual failures had to be hidden for fear of being booted out of the club themselves. Those weren't Christian churches. They were counterfeits using the name. They were not communities of disciples. They were collections of spiritual neurotics.

The notion that a local church should be a relational community of sinners in process of recovering the human stature God originally intended them to bear scares some people to death. An institutional church that judges and pretends and condemns is so much neater than a relational one that exists for spiritual transformation over time. The former assigns place. It tells who is "in" and who is "out." It ticks off formulas and tenets of orthodoxy. It often demands a degree of self-righteousness even to participate. Thus it requires isolation and secrets. And it turns the notion of church as Family of God into a grossly dysfunctional family where nobody can feel safe enough to tell the truth.

A man told me he had been caught pulling up pornography on his home computer. His wife hit the roof—as she had every right to do. She went to a couple of elders she knew her husband held in high regard to get their help. This was their notion of "helping" him. They went to the other elders of the church and told them what Sam (not his real name!) had done. They called Sam in for a meeting. They told him he could no longer teach his Sunday school class, would no longer be allowed to lead prayer at the church, and needed to make a public confession of sin to the church. He did so the very next Sunday and said something about "not setting a good example" and wanting forgiveness and prayers "from anyone I might have offended." Sounds like a good ending to a bad situation, right? No. It was actually a terrible mishandling of what could have been seized as a redemptive opportunity. It was an exercise in the "institutional processing" of what might have been a relational triumph for a man and his family—if the Spirit of God has been leading it.

In the conversation we had, it became apparent pretty quickly that Sam's problem isn't Internet pornography. Oh, it's a problem. But it is a symptom of something far deeper and more sinister. Sam has been involved in an affair with a woman at his workplace for the past seven months or so. He has been so absorbed in his guilt over what he is doing that he has started drinking some—for the first time since high school. When his wife caught him at the porn site in the wee hours that morning, he hadn't been able to sleep. He slipped out of bed and had a couple of drinks. He fired up his computer. That's when everything blew up in his face. He is publicly humiliated. The larger church body is backing his wife in her anger at him. And the only compassion he is getting is from the woman with whom he needs to end a guilt-laden affair. Want to guess where that scenario will end?

What if things had been handled differently? What if all the "facts of the case" were exactly the same until the time the woman went to her trusted elders? What if they had gone to Sam privately to confront him? What if he had been offered confidential help in dealing with whatever was going on? I can imagine Sam telling one of those elders who knew him personally what he poured out to me about what was really going on in his out-of-control life—and begging for somebody to help him figure out what to do. Out of the limelight of public humiliation, he and his wife might have found a way to salvage their marriage. With more concern for

Sam and his family than for the church's image "if anybody found out," those leaders could have become confessors and mentors. They could have dealt with him like they would have treated a brother or child in their nuclear families.

Do I defend Sam? Not for a minute. Do I know things would have turned out better if those elders had treated him differently? No. But my father and my two brothers would never have treated me that way if I had stolen money from the family store or hurt my wife. They would have treated me like family—because we *are* family—and tried helping before punishing. Alcoholics Anonymous could teach churches something about "intervention" with drunks that we could use with great value in dealing with our own drunks, philandering spouses, and other sinners. As a matter of fact, AA's intervention strategy is taken right from the Bible and follows its directions about dealing with broken relationships (Matt. 18:15-18). But Matthew 18 presumes that we are functioning relationally rather than institutionally. Are we?

From Isolation to Community

The world at large is fragmented and disconnected. It tends to emphasize differences and to enjoy creating situations of exclusion. Relationships are often cold and formal. People are increasingly competitive and violent. Anger seems to be the most common emotion on display. Mobility and urban sprawl—coupled with the fear of a knock on the door—have all but destroyed neighborhood ties.

Marriage pledges are not sacred. Children and parents live as strangers to each other—with each generation hiding things from the other. Symptoms of personal confusion ranging from chemical dependency to criminal behavior to suicide confront us on a daily basis.

Sociologists have described a phenomenon in American culture that Robert Bellah calls "ontological individualism." By this term he names the belief that each individual is her own source of meaning. Half a century ago, this spirit surfaced in religion in what came to be known as the Jesus Movement. It repudiated the role of the church in authentic spiritual life. It produced spiritual individualists without social attachments or corporate life. The pseudotheology that emerged from the movement offered what one author dubbed a "home correspondence course in salvation."

That spirit ran aground rather quickly. It not only runs counter to the New Testament vision of salvation but contradicts a fundamental need of human beings to live in community—a Christ-centered community of acceptance, accountability, and nurture where gradual spiritual transformation can take place over time. Although salvation is personal and individual in the sense of God's loving call to and acceptance of each person by name, it most certainly is not a private affair. While God saves individuals rather than groups, every saved individual is immediately incorporated into the Body of Christ. Anyone born from above is simultaneously born into the Family of God.

In *The Cross of Christ*, John Stott expressed it this way: "[T]he very purpose of his self-giving on the cross was not just to save isolated individuals, and so perpetuate their loneliness, but to create a new community whose members would belong to him, love one another and eagerly serve the world."[1]

God has existed from eternity past in the perfect communion of the Holy Trinity. The Christian God is not Aristotle's singular individual thinking thoughts of himself but a personal God in ideal fellowship. Created as we are in the image of God, we are created not only for fellowship with Father, Son, and Holy Spirit but for fellowship with one another as well. People need to belong, to fit in, and to be accepted. Everyone needs to sense that he or she is a significant member of a larger community. Of all people, the church as the Family of God should be able to give this message to one another. Accepted by God, we accept one another. We love one another. We hold one another accountable. We encourage one another. No castes. No favoritism. No discrimination. *And the medium becomes the message!*

We are the community of the children of God. We carry his spiritual DNA. We bear his name. We have a great inheritance. Awareness of these things makes a difference in how we see ourselves and function in this world. There is a Fred Craddock story that I love so much that I tell it often. It illustrates the difference it can make in a person's self-image and ability to function in this world when he is affirmed as a child of God.

Craddock and his wife were on vacation in the Great Smoky Mountains and had gone to the Black Bear Inn for dinner. They spotted an older man working the room and going from table to table. In his inimitable style, Craddock admits to hoping that the fellow would leave him alone. Sure enough, though, the man wound up at the vacationing couple's table, found out Craddock was a Christian Church minister, and pulled up a chair to join them. "I owe a great deal to a minister of the Christian Church," he said. The man began his story:

> I grew up in these mountains. My mother was not married, and the whole community knew it. I was what was called an illegitimate child. In those days that was a shame, and I was ashamed. The reproach that fell on her, of course, fell also on me. When I went into town with her, I could see people staring at me, making guesses as to who was my father. At school the children said ugly things to me, and so I stayed to myself during recess, and I ate my lunch alone.
>
> In my early teens I began to attend a little church back in the mountains called Laurel Springs Christian Church. It had a minister who was both attractive and frightening. He had a chiseled face and a heavy beard and a deep voice. I went to hear him preach. I don't know exactly why, but it did something for me. However, I was afraid that I was not welcome since I was, as

> they put it, a bastard. So I would go just in time for the sermon, and when it was over I would move out because I was afraid that someone would say, "What's a boy like you doing in a church?"
>
> One Sunday some people queued up in the aisle before I could get out, and I was stopped. Before I could make my way through the group, I felt a hand on my shoulder, a heavy hand. It was that minister. I cut my eyes around and caught a glimpse of his beard and his chin, and I knew who it was. I trembled in fear. He turned his face around so he could see mine and seemed to be staring for a little while. I knew what he was doing. He was going to make a guess as to who my father was. A moment later he said, "Well, boy, you're a child of . . . " and he paused there. And I knew it was coming. I knew I would have my feelings hurt. I knew I would not go back again. He said, "Boy, you're a child of God. I see a striking resemblance, boy." Then he swatted me on the bottom and said, "Now, you go claim your inheritance." I left the building a different person. In fact, that was really the beginning of my life.[2]

The preacher on vacation in the Smokies had really not wanted to be bothered by the old fellow. Now he was fascinated by what had just been shared with him. He was deeply moved and asked, "What's your name, sir?" Only then did he learn that he was talking with the former Republican Governor of Tennessee from 1911–1915, Ben Walter Hooper. The *Tennessee Blue Book* says of him that "Hooper's term saw child labor laws and compulsory school laws passed." Sounds like the man who had suffered so as a left-out and looked-over child wanted to protect some children from suffering when he could.

Perhaps if more of us saw ourselves as children of God rather than as members of the church, we would claim a nobler inheritance. If we understood church as persons in relationship rather than names on the roll, we would function differently as the church. If we saw sin as the breaking of relationships rather than the breaking of rules, we would both live better and deal with one another more gracefully.

The One-Another Texts

If we really love God the Father, we will create churches that are communities of love, accountability, and nurture where gradual spiritual transformation can occur over time. We will live gently with one another. Listen to one another's stories. Teach and learn from one another. Just think of some of those "one another" passages in the New Testament[3] that describe the ongoing activities of the church as the Family of God (quoted from NIV, italics added):

- "A new command I give you: *Love one another*. As I have loved you, so you must love one another. By this all men will know that you are my disciples, if you *love one another*" (John 13:34–35; see Rom. 13:8,10).
- "*Accept one another*, then, just as Christ accepted you, in order to bring praise to God" (Rom. 15:7).
- "I myself am convinced, my brothers, that you yourselves are full of goodness, complete in knowledge and competent to *instruct [give advice to, counsel] one another*" (Rom. 15:14).
- "Therefore *encourage one another* and *build each other up*, just as in fact you are doing" (1 Thess. 5:11).
- "*Carry one another's burdens*, and in this way you will fulfill the law of Christ" (Gal. 6:2).
- "*Be kind and compassionate to one another, forgiving each other*, just as in Christ God forgave you" (Eph. 4:32).
- "Therefore *confess your sins to each other* and *pray for each other* so that you may be healed" (James 5:16).

- "And let us consider how we may *spur one another on toward love and good deeds*" (Heb. 10:24).
- "Above all, *love each other deeply*, because love covers over a multitude of sins" (1 Pet. 4:8).

Does anyone doubt that the church would have far greater credibility with our not-yet-Christian neighbors if we modeled this sort of behavior consistently? Do you question that these positive relational activities count for more than our abilities to sing or preach or prove ourselves correct to those not-yet-Christians? Do you deny that we have been our own worst enemies over the years in neglecting these relational demands of our faith?

Sometimes naïvely pictured as the happy, unintended result of simply being together occasionally, Christian fellowship has to be nurtured intentionally. Resisting "ontological individualism," we must allow the Spirit to put on display the community qualities of the people of God.

The huge sequoia trees of California tower as much as three hundred feet above the ground. Strangely, though, they have unusually shallow root systems that extend in all directions to capture the maximum amount of surface moisture. For this reason, you seldom see one standing alone. High winds topple them quickly. So they grow in clusters. Their intertwined roots provide support against storms. Surely there is an insight here for the way God intends for the church to function as family. While no one is strong enough to withstand life's storms alone, our "one another" connectedness provides support. The Family of God is a propping-up community for its people.

In his Epistle to the Colossians, Paul expressed his concern that believers were in danger of being taken "captive through hollow and deceptive philosophy, which depends on human tradition and the basic principles of this world rather than on Christ" (2:8 NIV). Specifically, he warned them against letting anyone bind religious tests about things they could eat or drink or holidays they could or could not observe (2:16), and other "human commands and teachings" (2:23)—the very sorts of things institutional religion majors in doing! To the contrary, he urged them to fix their hearts on Jesus alone (3:1–4). Yes, some behaviors are to be avoided for the simple reason that they disrupt healthy relationships—lust and the sexual immorality it produces (3:5a); greed and the idolatry it generates (3:5b); anger and harsh judgments (3:8–9); and racism and elitism (3:11).

Finally, he makes his positive case for the kind of life Christians should live as the Family of God:

> Therefore, as God's chosen people, holy and dearly loved, clothe yourselves with compassion, kindness, humility, gentleness and patience. Bear with each other and forgive whatever grievances you may have against one another. Forgive as the Lord forgave you. And over all these virtues put on love, which binds them all together in perfect unity.
>
> Let the peace of Christ rule in your hearts, since as members of one body you were called to peace. And be thankful. Let the word of Christ dwell in you richly as you teach and admonish one another with all wisdom, and as you sing psalms, hymns and spiritual songs with gratitude in your hearts to God. And whatever you do, whether in word or deed, do it all in the name of the Lord Jesus, giving thanks to God the Father through him. (Col. 3:12–17 NIV)

Because of its appropriateness as a description of family life for Christians, I frequently use this text as a final charge to couples at their weddings. It is a call to love and respect, consideration and kindness. It describes the sort of healthy relationships that allow growth and spiritual formation, that confer peace and joy. And it describes a New Church for a New World that puts the heart of God on display in the relational life of his family.

"How great is the love the Father has lavished on us, that we should be called children of God!" exclaimed John the apostle. "And that is what we are!" (1 John 3:1 NIV). There is no greater honor to which a human can aspire. To be part of the Family of God. To have him as our Father. To be a member of the household of faith. To sit at the table where there is always abundance. To be where there is always room for others.

Who wouldn't want to be part of that experience?

Chapter Six

BUT TODAY IS THE SABBATH!

"Tradition is the living faith of the dead; traditionalism is the dead faith of the living."
—JAROSLAV PELIKAN

In an interview with a national news magazine several years ago, historian Jaroslav Pelikan—who taught on the faculty at Yale University from 1962 to 1996 and authored more than thirty books related to his discipline—said:

> Tradition is the living faith of the dead; traditionalism is the dead faith of the living. Tradition lives in conversation with the past, while remembering we are where and when we are and that it is we who have to decide. Traditionalism supposes that nothing should ever be done for the first time, so all that is needed to solve any problem is to arrive at the supposedly unanimous testimony of this homogenized tradition.[1]

There is a text in the Gospel of John that comes to mind in connection with this quote. It is a miracle account from Jesus' life that elicited censure rather than celebration, opposition to Jesus rather than adoration of him.

To be sure, this information about the healing of a paralyzed man, the challenge to Jesus about what he had done, and his response to the indictment can be appealed to for several important lessons. One could simply stress the importance of doing more to imitate Jesus' concern for the sick, vulnerable, and suffering. One could pursue the theme of spiritual sickness, blindness, and insensitivity over against a man's unresponsive limbs. Or one could trace out with great profit the bold claims Jesus makes for himself as the Son of God in the exchange with his critics. But the story also illustrates how easy it is for religion to get in God's way.

Religion Can Get in God's Way

Every individual, every family, and every religious group develops traditions. From personal reading habits to special holiday meals to focus areas for ministry, we evolve time-honored and customary ways of doing things. So far, so good. We need these habits and routines. They define us. They introduce our children into a culture. They help us know how to respond to challenges and new circumstances. They give us a sense of continuity with the past, a sense of depth, a sense of secure belonging. As Tevye says in *Fiddler on the Roof*: "Because of our traditions, everyone knows who he is and what God expects him to do."

Ah, but Tevye puts his finger on the problem with evolved human traditions in that same statement. Traditions are valuable. They steady and comfort us. But they are *not* always sacred divine expectations. They must sometimes yield to the exigency of new situations. Family rituals may, for example, become onerous and divisive rather than stabilizing if they don't change as family members alter their life situations. Children go off to college. Marriage demands the blending of two sets of family traditions. Grandchildren are born. Each of these situations demands a reshaping of rituals—or there can be real trouble. An inflexible soul who insists that everything must be kept as it always has been will soon be resented—even if catered to—by all parties involved. Someone is making a valued tradition into a soul-shriveling, anger-generating, absence-fostering traditionalism. What once helped stabilize a family can become a medium to destabilize it.

The same thing can be said about tradition versus traditionalism in religion. Leith Anderson tells the story of a Danish Lutheran church where people filed in, walked to the front of the center aisle, and—facing a plain white wall—reverently bowed. Then each worshipper took his or her regular seat. A visitor was curious enough about the ritual to ask for an explanation, but neither laity nor clergy in the church seemed to know the origin of or justification for the practice.

With the curiosity of several aroused now, further research revealed that there was an elaborate painting of the Virgin Mary behind the layers of white paint on the blank wall. That painting dated back several hundred years to a time before the Protestant Reformation when the structure was a Roman Catholic worship center. When the church became Protestant and the painting was covered over, the worshippers just kept coming in and bowing. Generations later, the practice was still being perpetuated—even though the reason had long since been forgotten. Such is the power of religious tradition.

Some of the religious people in Jesus' time were so caught up in their traditions that they could no longer distinguish an event from its purpose, the original justification from its accustomed performance. Animal sacrifice, Sabbath, and tithing were originally God's ideas taught to his human creatures. The mistake certain Jewish religionists made was to retain the form without the substance. And Jesus rebuked them with these words: "Go and learn what this means: 'I desire mercy, not sacrifice'" (Matt. 9:13 NIV; see Hos. 6:6).

Traditions Over People

Here is a case study in Jewish experience from the first century that should help people of our own time understand the difference between following Jesus and defending the trappings and customs of the Christian religion.

John uses the episode with incredible skill to declare God's intention to use form and tradition to bless rather than burden his creatures. Sabbath, worship rituals, tithing, sacrifice—all these external trappings of faith taught through Moses had been designed to bring God's love into the lives of people, not to regulate their behaviors and make God's presence into an oppressive weight.

My one trip to Jerusalem several years ago included a visit to the pool in this story. Scholars had wondered for generations how it was configured so as to have "five porticoes." When it was unearthed years ago, the mystery came clear. It was a huge, huge pool—bisected by an interior porch. In other words, it looked like two big, rectangular pools put end to end. So the complete structure had the expected four porticoes, with one per side, plus a fifth that cut across and reduced the distance one would have to traverse to walk around it completely. Here is what happened there one day:

> After this there was a festival of the Jews, and Jesus went up to Jerusalem.
>
> Now in Jerusalem by the Sheep Gate there is a pool, called in Hebrew Beth-zatha, which has five porticoes. In these lay many invalids—blind, lame, and paralyzed. One man was there who had been ill for thirty-eight years. When Jesus saw him lying there and knew that he had been there a long time, he said to him, "Do you want to be made well?" The sick man answered him, "Sir, I have no one to put me into the pool when the water is stirred up; and while I am making my way, someone else steps down ahead of me." Jesus said to him, "Stand up, take your mat and walk." At once the man was made well, and he took up his mat and began to walk.
>
> Now that day was a sabbath. (John 5:1–10a)

What an event! A man paralyzed for thirty-eight years was walking home under his own power, with his beggar's mat tucked under his arm! But some bystanders from a Taliban-like Ministry for the Promotion of Virtue and Elimination of Vice saw him and challenged his right to be carrying something on a holy day. "It is the sabbath," they told him. "It is not lawful for you to carry your mat" (5:10b). When the poor fellow replied that he was just doing what the healer had told him to do, the protectors of orthodoxy set out to get clear on this healer's identity. It was discovered that Jesus was the healer in question, and John informs us: "Therefore the Jews started persecuting Jesus, because he was doing such things on the sabbath" (5:16).

Incredible! A man whose limbs had been immobile for thirty-eight years was well, and the legalistic religionists of Jerusalem set out to persecute Jesus rather than to praise him, learn from him, and further his ministry of compassion. And can you visualize this situation from the perspective of the healed man? His life had just been transformed by Jesus, but the joy of that event was about to be overshadowed by the legalistic traditionalism he had been challenged to debate.

Jesus began his response to the hidebound religionists by saying, "My Father is still working, and I also am working" (5:17). God sustains the cosmos constantly. He is sovereign over all people and all things without taking any time off. So, since Jesus is God incarnate, he asserted that he has every right to be who he is and to do what his nature calls him to do at any time. He wasn't "breaking the sabbath" but simply being who he was and showing compassion to a lame man. He was also modeling the truth for mortal onlookers that the Sabbath rules had never been designed to prohibit kindness.

But are we reading too much into this to see his reference to "My Father" as a claim to deity for himself? Indeed not. The people present that day understood it so, and he didn't take it back or disclaim their interpretation of his words.

> But Jesus answered them, "My Father is still working, and I also am working." For this reason the Jews were seeking all the more

> to kill him, because he was not only breaking the sabbath, but was also calling God his own Father, thereby making himself equal to God.
>
> Jesus said to them, "Very truly, I tell you, the Son can do nothing on his own, but only what he sees the Father doing; for whatever the Father does, the Son does likewise. The Father loves the Son and shows him all that he himself is doing; and he will show him greater works than these, so that you will be astonished. Indeed, just as the Father raises the dead and gives them life, so also the Son gives life to whomever he wishes." (John 5:17–21)

Jesus or Religion?

Unless we get over some of our hang-ups about religion, we are going to continue missing Jesus. We won't see him. We won't understand his words. We won't be able to share him with others—and we will, indeed, get in the way of his effort to make himself known to them.

Yes, we must honor and live within the limits of Scripture. We must regard the written Word of God as authoritative. It is the single document in all the world that is God-breathed and capable of making known his will for our lives. Having said that, however, we must not forget that Scripture is not an end in itself. It is meant to point us to Jesus in his personhood and to call us into a personal relationship with him. But if we are not very, very careful, Scripture can become an end instead of a means. We will fight scholarly battles over texts and tenses and put out each other's eyes until neither of us can see Jesus. Yet we may both feel holy for having fought!

That is what Jesus told the people present the day he healed the paralyzed man: "You search the scriptures because you think that in them you have eternal life; and it is they that testify on my behalf. Yet you refuse to come to me to have life" (John 5:39–40).

Jesus' fiercest opposition came from religious leaders who viewed him as a threat to their ability to run the religious establishment. They were respected theologians who had studied for years and who had built up a following of sincere students. I suspect most of them had good motives—at least originally. But they had become the enemies of Jesus. The most forbidding barrier between Jesus Christ and all those he would heal from their spiritual ailments is still the traditionalism attached to religion.

It is time to choose presence over ritual, the living Jesus over mere church membership. It is time for us to seek and affirm spirituality lived in relationship with Jesus rather than Christianity defined by denomination or traditionalism. It is high time to learn the meaning of Christ's challenge about mercy over sacrifice. Rather than leave the challenge of this text vague for you, let me underscore three very practical consequences of understanding its message.

Three Insights

Inclusion. The Pharisees of Jesus' day and the traditionalists-legalists of every generation work to make outsiders feel uncomfortable and unwanted; Jesus is eager to accept those outsiders. Jesus was intentional about associating with people the religionists of his time considered untouchable. Jesus' church has not always followed his lead, choosing instead to be an insulated community behind walls and stained glass windows. If Jesus is light and if he has sent us into the world bearing witness to him, there is no need to fear darkness. There is certainly no justification for the self-righteousness that avoids people such as drug addicts or persons with HIV/AIDS because their suffering has been self-inflicted.[2]

Affirmation. The religionists of Jesus' time valued their traditions over people; Jesus always valued people for the image of God he saw in them. People who are wed to institutional custom, whether then or now, persist in stressing the letter of the law and trying to dispense the artesian well of God's redemptive grace through the soda straw of their neat theological systems. A prime example of this would be the way our human zeal to protect marriage has made divorced and remarried persons feel like second-class Christians—if they are convinced they can be Christians at all.

Relationship. Organized religion—whether Judaism or Christianity—trusts its rules; Jesus offers people a relationship. While the animal sacrifices of Amos' time and during Jesus' earthly ministry were commanded by God, many of the worshippers were convinced sacrifice was a way to buy God's favor rather than merely a grateful response to his love. Sacrifice never was the basis for approaching God, and those who understood and practiced it as such were guilty of reducing an intimate relationship to a legalistic formula. Legalists fear that an overemphasis on God's love and grace will lead to license, but they are the ones who—by focusing on formulas, right actions, and church rituals—are presuming on God's grace. And Jesus was incredibly stern with such persons.

Religion put Jesus to death once. Then it did it again. And again and again across time. It is time to put away human-controlled, rule-bounded, life-stifling religion for the sake of letting him live in a world that needs him so desperately.

Chapter Seven

CAUGHT RED-HANDED!

"God invented forgiving
as a remedy for a past
not even he could change
and not even he could forget."
—LEWIS B. SMEDES

How many fairy tales, songs, books, and movies have the following story line? There is a beautiful girl who was born to be a princess. Her heart is pure. Her love is true. But, alas! She is in the clutches of some evil person or malevolent curse. She is trapped and unattainable. Her only hope is that a strong and handsome prince will come to set her free. But he will have to be both physically powerful and spiritually pure to enter her world, defeat her captor, and win her hand.

Just as she is beginning to despair of her prince, he appears. With daring and skill, he lays siege to the tower and the sinister force holding her. Much blood is shed. The knight on his powerful steed is beaten back once and again. But he rises and fights. Eventually the sorcerer is defeated, the dragon is slain, or the villain is destroyed. The object of such heroism and valor is rescued. Her heart is captured by him forever. And they ride off to his cottage in the woods—or castle on the hill—to live happily ever after.

After envisioning just such a scenario, John Eldredge writes:

> Why is this story so deep in our psyche? Every little girl knows the fable without ever being told. She dreams one day her prince will come. Little boys rehearse their part with wooden swords and cardboard shields. And one day the boy, now a young man, realizes that he wants to be the one to win the beauty. Fairy tales, literature, music, and movies all borrow from this mythic theme. Sleeping Beauty, Cinderella, Helen of Troy, Romeo and Juliet, Antony and Cleopatra, Arthur and Guinevere, Tristan and Isolde. From ancient fables to the latest blockbuster, the theme of a strong man coming to rescue a beautiful woman is universal to human nature. It is written in our hearts, one of the core desires of every man and every woman.[1]

If there is any truth at all to this claim, how devastating it must be for a woman to receive the opposite message. She is not valued. She is not desired. There is no one who will fight for her. She is not the cherished treasure of anyone. She is ugly and undesirable, coarse and uncouth, unloved and abhorrent. Know what will happen to that woman? Practically every horrible thing you can imagine. And she will tell herself that she deserves those things. If she is abused or abandoned as a child, she is likely to do most anything as an adult just to get attention that she will call "love." She will let men insult, harass, and assault her—emotionally, physically, and sexually—and it will never occur to her that she deserves anything else. At that point in her history, it is unlikely that her hero will appear. She has lost her innocent charm. Her beauty has been compromised long since. She no longer thinks she deserves a prince, for it has been forever and a day since she has been anyone's princess.

From Fiction to Fact

We meet such a woman in the Gospel of John. She is compromised. She has committed an awful sin. Though self-judgment has led to her situation, she is now facing judgment from the biblical scholars before whom she has been exposed. Then the woman and her accusers meet Jesus.

> Then each of them went home, while Jesus went to the Mount of Olives. Early in the morning he came again to the temple. All the people came to him and he sat down and began to teach them. The scribes and the Pharisees brought a woman who had been caught in adultery; and making her stand before all of them, they said to him, "Teacher, this woman was caught in the very act of committing adultery. Now in the law Moses commanded us to stone such women. Now what do you say?" They said this to test him, so that they might have some charge to bring against him. Jesus bent down and wrote with his finger on the ground. When they kept on questioning him, he straightened up and said to them, "Let anyone among you who is without sin be the first to throw a stone at her." And once again he bent down and wrote on the ground. When they heard it, they went away, one by one, beginning with the elders; and Jesus was left alone with the woman standing before him. Jesus straightened up and said to her, "Woman, where are they? Has no one condemned you?" She said, "No one, sir." And Jesus said, "Neither do I condemn you. Go your way, and from now on do not sin again." (John 7:53–8:11)

This story of the adulteress is almost certainly a late, non-Johannine addition to the fourth Gospel. Most English translations since the King James Version indicate as much by breaking the text with space, brackets, or a different typeface. Some put it as a footnote. All explain that these twelve verses are absent from the oldest manuscripts of the Gospel of John.

Critical commentaries are unanimous in observing that the vocabulary and style of these verses differ considerably from the remainder of the Gospel of John and are more like one of the Synoptics. As a matter of fact, one family of New Testament manuscripts places this story after Luke 21:38.

The fairest judgment is simply to say that we have come to a story that was not originally a part of this Gospel but whose traditional place has come to be John 7:53–8:11. It was preserved in extracanonical writings as a piece of authentic tradition from the life of Jesus. Rescued from its independent wanderings, it finally found its way into the canonical text here. Several scholars have conjectured it was inserted here to illustrate Jesus' words recorded at 8:15: "I judge no one."

This Story Tells Me . . .

The sad plight of a woman caught in adultery turns into a beautiful story about compassion and the opportunity for a new beginning. It has critical, historical, and interpretive challenges worth pursuing in graduate school. But I am a theologian and teacher who meets people like this woman practically every day. They are men and women who have been hurt and made cynical by life. They are people who may have stopped caring. They are women who are guilty of things they are embarrassed to name. They are men who deserve to die, want to die, and may have tried to die. I love what this story tells me to tell them.

This text informs me that I am not playing fast and loose with the Bible to tell someone who has committed sin that he can still be forgiven. I can even tell someone who has committed an embarrassing and known-to-everybody sexual sin that she can have a second chance and start over. I can feel confident in telling people that the real issue in their lives is not their past in sin but their future with God.

When I tell people that, some of them can't believe it. It's just too good to be true. It flies in the face of everything they've been told before. It is different from the message given them by some church somewhere. But the church doesn't always say the same thing Jesus says, and *Jesus is the benchmark for truth.* Jesus takes precedence over tradition. Jesus triumphs over biblical interpretation. Jesus' constant mercy can be trusted over Christianity's occasional heartlessness.

Marnie Ferree is a dear friend of mine. And Marnie is a professional counselor who—with her husband David's support and encouragement—ministers Christ's healing message to people with a past. Know what drew Marnie to her ministry? Know what taught her compassion for women like the one in this text? She has been there herself—and, by the healing grace of Jesus Christ, has come back to tell her story of redemption.

> I knew how the world dealt with women like me. I'd heard the jokes about loose women. I'd experienced the revolving door of exploitation on the one hand and condemnation on the other. I knew the world saw me as a loser, but I didn't really care about the people of the world.
>
> It was the religious folk I was afraid of. The Christians—the church people—those were the ones I wanted to avoid. I knew how the church dealt with sinners like me. They still threw stones. Maybe not literal ones, but sharp ones nonetheless.
>
> Stones of gossip. I'd heard the whispers and the rumors.
>
> Stones of withdrawal. I'd seen the averted eyes, the retreating backs. People avoided me. Who wants to associate with a woman caught in adultery?
>
> Stones of judgment. The condemnation overwhelmed me. I try not to blame the religious folk. Most thought judging me was the right thing to do. Good Christians are supposed to take a strong stand against sin.
>
> All I knew was that those stones didn't help. The threat of punishment sure wasn't turning my life around. Yes, I was afraid of hell, but I was already living in it, and I didn't know a way out. I knew everything about rules. I had no clue about relationship.

Until I encountered Jesus. His approach was totally different and surprising. He was kind with me and gentle. He looked tenderly into my soul and saw my pain. He saw my past and how desperately I wanted a different future. He knew I couldn't do it on my own, and He didn't expect me to. He offered forgiveness. He showered me with grace. He caught me with His love and threw His power against my pain.

Jesus gave me hope for the future and grace for the journey. Instead of beating me up with stones, He challenged me with His love. He called me to a different life. He led me to the resources that made it possible. He coaxed me into relationship.

And one day at a time, by the grace of my Savior, this sinful, sexually addicted woman has been walking with Him in a newness of life.

It's not stones that help the sinner. It's only a relationship with a Savior.[2]

Why Some Doubt God's Mercy

The claim "God really loves you" falls on stony hearts with some people. Whether caught red-handed or wrestling alone in the night with their guilt, they cannot find it in themselves to look toward God. It isn't so much that they don't believe in God and his love, I suspect, as it reflects some painful things out of their past that have made them doubt there is such a loving and benevolent Creator of all things who cares about them. Life, you see, has a way of inflicting some terribly painful wounds on human hearts. God is often presented as having a less-than-friendly heart for sinners. Sometimes pain and abuse are inflicted on people in his name. And Satan tries to use those hurts as wedges between people and God. Let me explain.

The Golden Text of the Bible says this: "For God so loved the world that he gave his one and only Son, that whoever believes in him shall not perish but have eternal life" (John 3:16 NIV). That verse plays beautiful, positive notes of music in my heart. I know what it is to be loved by someone (e.g., father, mother, wife, children), and I can transfer those positive notions to God. I can imagine the positive, affirming attitude of God toward me and calculate some of the positive effects of such a love in my life.

"As a mother comforts her child, so will I comfort you" (Isa. 66:13 NIV). I can identify with that image of God because of experiences with my mother when I was so sick for so many years as a child. "But while [the prodigal son] was still a long way off, his father saw him and was filled with compassion for him; he ran to his son, threw his arms around him and kissed him" (Luke 15:20 NIV). I know I disappointed my father in some situations, but he never turned against me or cut me out of his life. So I can identify with these positive images of God's parental role in my life. And so on for biblical metaphors about Christ loving the church as a husband loves his wife, my unqualified love for my daughter and two sons, and the meaning of friends and other affirming persons in my life.

But there are some people who no longer believe in love because they have been hurt and exploited in the name of "love." Maybe some of those factors were at work in the background of the biblical narrative cited above. A woman was molested as a child by some man who pretended to love her. Or she was a teenager or young adult when somebody said he loved her and then dumped her and left her behind—maybe with children to care for by herself.

A man is defrauded by business partners he thought were his friends. Someone's memories of childhood involve an abusive parent who scolded, berated, or beat him in the name of "loving" him. People have been betrayed by preachers who—in the name of "God's love"—built little empires or practiced their immoral behaviors behind a smokescreen of piety. If the word "love" conjures up negative memories, painful images, and thoughts of defective relationships, talk about God's love can be barren or painful.

Others cannot believe in God's love, for they were taught that God has been the source of all their heartache. Maybe they heard, "God took your baby because he wanted him more than you did," or "God gave you that brain tumor to teach you to trust him." A brokenhearted lady confided in me about her confusion and anger at God over a severely handicapped and mentally retarded child. Some people from a church near her had told her, "God gives children with such special needs only to very special mothers who can give them what they need." Though I'm sure those people meant well by their pious sentiment, what they didn't know was that her health was beginning to break under the strain and that her husband had just told her that he couldn't take it anymore and was leaving. Did God arrange those things for her because she was capable of handling "special" situations?

What reasonable person can believe in a loving God if he or she has been taught to think that bankruptcy and heart attacks, car wrecks and divorces, or handicapped children and deserting husbands are his way of singling people out for tragedy? Why, the legalese of insurance policies and the frequent language of people on the street both label tornadoes, fires, floods, and the like "acts of God"! An accumulation of tragic events coupled with an interpretation that lays them at the feet of God could cause people to hate and blaspheme him. At the very least, it would be hard for those people to hear "God loves you" as a meaningful statement.

Maybe they are angry at life in general because they've had such a hard time. Perhaps they are angry at themselves for ruining what was once a fairly decent life. So God has become their "whipping boy," for he seems to be a fairly safe punching bag for much of our human disappointment and rage. It's like an angry child screaming at her Mommy because she doesn't know what else to do with her anger. People sometimes scream at or indict God because they are in more pain than they think they can bear, and they simply must strike out in one direction or another.

So I cannot assume that everybody I meet feels kindly disposed toward God. From a wide variety of life experiences, he may have very ambivalent feelings toward God's love. She may not believe in God at all because of her secular worldview. He may be so confused by what he has seen and heard from Christians that it is impossible to make sense of (much less believe!) the words "God loves you very, very much."

When I try to be Jesus in that person's life and help him in the midst of his pain, it may backfire on me. If you'll pardon the analogy, it is sometimes like trying to rescue a bird with a broken wing or a puppy who has been hit by a car. Try to pick up the bird, and he'll peck at you and make angry sounds. Try to examine the dog's broken leg, and he'll snap at you—and bite you, if he can.

The one thing Christ's followers must not do is use the anger, ingratitude, or negative responses of some of the people we try to help as our excuse for withholding compassion and love. The job of the church is to make God's love believable by treating people with respect, care, and support—even, no especially, the "hard cases."

The Convincing Evidence

Ultimately, however, the proof of the love of God doesn't come from our attempts at imitating Jesus to the people among whom we live but in telling the story of God's dealings with humanity across the centuries. He is incredibly quick to compassion and slow to anger. He is eager to bless and reluctant to punish. "He is patient with you, not wanting anyone to perish, but everyone to come to repentance" (2 Pet. 3:9 NIV). Even when he must punish evil in order to defend not only his own integrity but also the integrity of those who are attempting to live in holiness, he does so with the option of grace always on the table. "You are forgiving and good, O Lord, abounding in love to all who call to you" (Ps. 86:5). People remember the terrible flood of purging waters that God sent over the Earth but are inclined to forget that he gave wicked humanity 120 years to repent and be spared. People remember the fiery end of Sodom and Gomorrah but seem to forget that if only ten people could have been found in those two cities who could grieve over their wickedness, both would have been spared.

Thank God that he is so gracious and compassionate, so slow to anger and abounding in love! Thank God that he "relents from sending calamity" when we make the slightest moves back to him!

Jonah ran from God because he was a bigot and racist, but God still pursued him. Hosea's wife was a prostitute, but Yahweh told Hosea to pursue her as he was still pursuing Israel. Noah got drunk, Jeremiah was depressed and suicidal, Elijah burned out. Moses stuttered, Naomi was a widow, and Samson (can you believe it!) was a man who had long hair. Both Moses and Paul had the blood of murders on their hands. Peter was afraid of dying, and Lazarus already had died. Miriam was a gossip, Martha was a neurotic worrier, and John could be self-righteous.

Why does God keep on pursuing people like these "losers"? Why does he keep on lavishing his love on me? Why is he trying to connect with your heart right now? It's because he loves you. He loves you very, very much. He really does!

To look with the eye of faith to see the cross of Jesus Christ settles all doubt. Augustine was right when he said the cross is a pulpit from which Jesus preached God's love to the world. "In this is love, not that we loved God but that he loved us and sent his Son as an atoning sacrifice for our sins" (1 John 4:10 NIV).

I once heard a teacher quote the text that follows and speak of "three strands" it weaves together from the biblical record: "You see, at just the right time, when we were still powerless, Christ died for the ungodly. Very rarely will anyone die for a righteous man, though for a good man someone might possibly dare to die. But God demonstrates his own love for us in this: While we were still sinners, Christ died for us" (Rom. 5:6–8 NIV).

First, the *crimson thread* ends the verse: "Christ died for us." What does that mean? There are mothers and fathers who would die for their children. You love your babies so much that you would gladly trade places if cancer or a car out of control was threatening your child's life. I've stood in hospital corridors more than once and heard people sob, "Why couldn't it have been me? I'd have gladly taken his place!" Do you hear the words: take his place, trade places, die for her? That's what Jesus did on the cross.

Second, there is a *stained thread* in this text: Christ died in our place "while we were still sinners." We weren't obedient, loving children when Jesus traded places with us and was put to death in our place. We were rebels. We were disobedient. We had not asked him to do anything for us because we were determined and deliberate in our sinfulness. Because of our sins, we deserved to die. Because he took our place that day, we can live. "The wages of sin is death, but the gift of God is eternal life in Christ Jesus our Lord" (Rom. 6:23 NIV). We didn't deserve it and hadn't asked for it. It was a gift to us in our pathetically dark, stained, sinful lives.

Third, there is a *golden thread* of divine love: "God demonstrates his own love for us in this." In some other settings and in light of some of your experiences, the message that God loves you very, very much can sound hollow, unconvincing, and even trite. But if you have been moved to see the cross of Jesus through the eye of faith, those words ring true. They hold the prospect of forgiveness and the beginning of a new life.

When You Are Caught Red-Handed

For people caught red-handed in any sin, there is only one hope. It isn't law. It isn't judgment. Often, unfortunately, it isn't the church or its leaders. It is brokenness, pardon, and a new beginning with Jesus.

This whole scene of the woman caught in adultery smacks of malice. Since lovers are discreet and cautious in their clandestine affairs, how could this woman have been "caught in the very act" of having adulterous sex with some man? She appears to have been used *twice* here—once by her sexual partner and again by the larger group that set a trap for her. It is clear that she had been set up as a test case for Jesus. The professional teachers of Scripture were going to check out his orthodoxy with this engaged or married woman who had broken her covenant of fidelity to her husband.

But wait just a minute. Where was the man? If she was caught "in the very act of committing adultery," there has to have been a man present. Was her paramour party to the entrapment? The Law of Moses would have required that both parties be put to death, but the scholars only brought the woman. Women have been subjected to a double standard in sexual mores and behaviors in every culture in history. Things that men do and brag about are often scandalous for women. Multiple sex partners make him an s-t-u-d; the same things make her an s-l-u-t.

So what about the Law's requirement to stone *somebody* here? The Law of Moses actually doesn't begin with stoning. It begins with the obligation to warn a sinner and offer encouragement for her to repent. Otherwise, the individual who knows of a person's sin shares in its guilt. "You shall not hate in your heart anyone of your kin; you shall reprove your neighbor, or you will incur guilt yourself" (Lev. 19:17). Had these accusers rebuked the woman and her lover? Or had they hidden, allowed the sin to occur without challenge, and come to Jesus rather than to the woman herself with their accusation?

When Jesus told those people, "Let anyone among you who is without sin be the first to throw a stone at her" (8:7b), he hung them out to dry—and they knew it. Our modern practice of "turning state's evidence" against a co-conspirator in a capital case is just that—a *modern* practice. The Law of Moses required not that one be "without sin" in the absolute sense (i.e., perfect in all matters) before giving testimony in a capital case but that the witness be "without sin" in the matter at hand (i.e., not a party to the act). Against the background of Exodus 23:1, a "malicious witness" was held to be not only the person who lied but a person who testified to the truth incompetently, from vengeful motives, or in collusion with someone bringing charges from a false motive. In the case of the woman caught in adultery, anyone who gave testimony or participated in this woman's stoning would thereby become subject to being stoned himself. Jesus snared them in their own net—for the sake of giving the woman a second chance.

Another Victory for Jesus over Religion

Her dashing, heroic prince *did* come! No fairy tale here. No cross-cultural myth preserving a little girl's need to be cherished and fought for. This is the real thing! This is the Prince of Light rescuing a hopeless, helpless woman from the Prince of Darkness—and giving her the opportunity to experience new life. This was not a rescue to romance; it was the ultimate rescue from lostness to life.

As the little pile of stones built up from being dropped to the ground while Jesus looked away—perhaps an act of face-saving mercy even for them—those same rocks became a monument to grace over law, life over death, Jesus over religion. The memory of those rocks on the ground is the hope the rest of us have for being treated the same way.

One of my early teachers and mentors was such a good man in so many ways. In unguarded moments spent with him, I saw occasional instances of what I believe was genuine compassion for hurting souls. But he was sometimes loyal to Christianity over Jesus and could be ruthless to people for the sake of upholding the "image of the church in the community." After we had gone our different theological and ministry paths, he felt compelled to rebuke me for becoming "soft with sin" in my work.

In a note that documents the distinction between the Jesus I know from the Gospels and the Jesus recast by Christian history, a deacon once challenged my eagerness to welcome seriously broken people into the life of our church. He asked: "What would people think of a church that is filled with alcoholics, adulterers, and divorced people?" Hoping to be direct without sounding arrogant or disrespectful, I could only respond by saying: "They might think we were the church Jesus promised to build."

To paraphrase Marnie: Rocks don't help us sinners, but Jesus does.

Chapter Eight

Learning to Play Well on the Road

"I am not here attacking Christianity, but only the institutional mantle that cloaks it."
—Pierre Berton

Any coach of any sport would tell you that the key to her or his team's success is its ability to play well on the road. Teams love to have home-field advantage, but the championship teams know how to perform in venues that are not their natural environs. Do you think there is anything to be learned here for the life of the church?

This book has tried to make a theological point by distinguishing between Jesus and Christianity. By now it should be obvious that one of the major issues involved in the distinction has to do with a post-Constantine penchant for the church to insulate itself from the world. Sometimes there are literal walls behind which the church has hidden itself. Think of monasteries or cloisters here. More often, however, the walls are ideological and practical. There is an us-versus-them mindset that creates sacred spaces for worship and uses language that makes a sharp distinction between what is done in those spaces at certain appointed times and what happens in "everyday life" or—even worse—"*real* life."

To a mindset that draws a sharp line between sacred and secular, that language is meaningful. But the best evidence is that Jesus did not draw the sharp line to which we are accustomed between the two. He saw the kingdom reign of God to be sovereign over all of life. Worship *is* real life, and every element of everyday life has a worshipful dimension.

Putting a wall between sacred and secular, holy and secular, or this-worldly concerns and other-worldly issues has had consequences. It has, for example, led us to think of "my personal spiritual life" over against "my public business life." Thus we debate whether politicians or athletes should ever have their fitness for acclaim (e.g., votes, a place in the Hall of Fame, etc.) measured by some moral shortcoming in their "private" lives. The consensus seems to be that there is no necessary connection between the two.

We speak with reverence about the "sacred space" we experience in a cathedral or sanctuary, at a retreat center or breathtaking spot in nature. The store or office or den is, one presumes, "secular space" for us. So we have created a religious environment in much of Christendom that allows people to participate in church events as pious, reverent members on Sunday morning—while being lecherous, racist, greedy, immoral, or criminal the other six and a half days of the week! Church is sacred; other settings are not. *Where did we get such absurd notions of the nature of reality?*

Life is continuous from church pew to classroom to golf course. There is a single narrative from Bible class to workplace to football stadium. Each of us is weaving a single tapestry with innermost thoughts to words from the tongue to behaviors in unguarded moments. How naïve to argue otherwise.

The late Abraham Heschel used to raise this question: Is it an artist's inner vision or her grappling with stone that creates a brilliant piece of sculpture? The point of his question was to say that upright living is like a work of art. It is the outcome of both an inner vision and a struggle with very concrete situations. "No religious act is properly fulfilled unless it is done with a willing heart and a craving soul," Heschel said. "You cannot worship God with your body if you do not know how to worship him with your soul."[1] And vice versa, one might add.

Worship as Sunday morning event or private time devotional is the easy part of Christian experience. It is where we sense home-field advantage, and there is little temptation to evil while in prayer or Bible study. Even so, a spiritual discipline such as prayer, Bible reading, or fasting is not meant to be an end in itself. We obey God not for the sake of achieving or earning but to keep our hearts open to him and responsive to his will.

When we take our faith on the road, though, there is more of a challenge. Outside the sanctuary and away from a group of affirming fellow-members, maintaining the integrity of one's faith does not happen apart from a clear intention. The key here is to jettison the notion of a bifurcated world—sacred here and secular there. *All* space—cathedral, sickroom, factory, mountain lake, farm, office cubicle, car, sidewalk, jail cell—is sacred to God. *All* places are where he can be sought and found. *All* may be dedicated to his glory by the use made of it. If God is with us and in us, how could it be otherwise?

All of Life Is Service to God

"All of life is worship!" people say. Well, not quite. Not as we use the word "worship" in contemporary settings, anyway.

For practically anyone who uses the word in a religious context—whether Catholic or Protestant, Muslim or Jew, atheist or agnostic—the term *worship* signifies a set of rituals or prayers or other acts of devotion directed toward a deity. That being the case, it just wouldn't be correct to say that everything one does is worship. During the past week, you likely washed dishes or cleaned gutters or changed a tire. You probably drove a car, bought something at a store, and opened mail. You certainly ate, brushed your teeth, and went to the bathroom. Perhaps you think of all those things as worshipful acts, but I doubt it. (I started to list sleeping, but some people *are* known to include that act in their regular practice of Sunday morning worship!)

I suspect most of us think of worship as what we do on Sunday mornings in assembly with others who share a common faith commitment. We meet at a designated place at a specified time. We stand and sit in unison. We read Scripture. We pray. These are times, places, and activities of corporate worship. There are, of course, many of us who also set times of personal or family worship in which we do some or all of the same things—usually for briefer periods of time and with more spontaneity to them. We would probably even say that some things are more appropriate to one place and time than another. But we would all know that this is the standard and customary meaning of the word. We worship when we deliberately set our minds to do so. We do certain customary things that express adoration of and commitment to our God.

The Bible uses the Hebrew and Greek words for worship in exactly the same way. So Abraham, Isaac, and two unnamed men traveled to Moriah. The two men were left to wait as the father and son went to a designated place to do a ritual thing. "Stay here with the donkey while I and the boy go over there," he told them. "We will worship and then we will come back to you" (Gen. 22:5 NIV). Yahweh made himself known to Moses through a burning bush at Mount Horeb and called him to lead the Israelites out of Egyptian bondage. "When you have brought the people out of Egypt," he told Moses, "you will worship God on this mountain" (Ex. 3:12). One day an angel sent the evangelist Philip to intersect an Ethiopian who was traveling back to his home. "This man had gone to Jerusalem to worship, and on his way home was sitting in his chariot reading the book of Isaiah the prophet" (Acts 8:27b–28). Biblical writers use the word just as we do to signify time and places, rituals and ceremonies.

Yet one also comes across a text such as this one in the Word of God: "Therefore, I urge you, brothers, in view of God's mercy, to offer your bodies as living sacrifices, holy and pleasing to God—this is your spiritual act of worship" (Rom. 12:1). Perhaps it is more precise to say, as earlier in this chapter, that every element of everyday life has a worshipful dimension. I actually prefer the translation of the term found here (in Greek, *latreía*[2]) in the King James and American Standard Versions. They use the word "service" instead.

With this much background and I hope not-too-tedious explanation for some key distinctions I think are appropriate, let me offer a statement for unpacking: *"All of life is service to God, and worship is how we stay focused on that mission."*

Every thought, word, and action in your life as a Christian—from washing dishes to cleaning gutters, from the way you drive on the highway to the way you treat the clerk who helps you in the store, from what you eat to the details of your personal hygiene—should be done as a statement of total-life apprenticeship to Jesus Christ.

If that isn't true, please explain where this biblical instruction fits into your life as a Christ-follower: "And whatever you do, whether in word or deed, do it all in the name of the Lord Jesus, giving thanks to God the Father through him" (Col. 3:17 NIV). Here is the same verse from the New Living Translation: "And whatever you do or say, let it be as a representative of the Lord Jesus, all the while giving thanks through him to God the Father." Finally, here is Eugene Peterson's paraphrase from *The Message*: "Let every detail in your lives—words, actions, whatever—be done in the name of the Master, Jesus, thanking God the Father every step of the way."

Paul said the same thing to Christians in the pagan culture of Corinth: "So whether you eat or drink or whatever you do, do it all for the glory of God" (1 Cor. 10:31 NIV). How personal do we dare to make this instruction in order to grasp its significance? Whether you are a physician or schoolteacher or hourly wage-earner, do it all for the glory of God—not in the grumbling, half-hearted, nobody-will-ever-know spirit of the world. Whether you live in the suburbs or the projects, live there for the glory of God—bearing witness to God's presence in your home. Whether you are single or married, enjoying good health or fighting cancer, enjoying your children or grieving that you cannot get pregnant, celebrating or brokenhearted—be who you are where you are today to the praise and glory of God.

I understand Romans 12:1 to say that our lives as God's people in a world still under the rule of the Prince of Darkness are supposed to bear witness to an alternate, better reality that we know about. The world is drinking from a poisoned well that makes it think and act insanely, and we are supposed to model sanity in its midst. We aren't here to judge the world and to scream at it. We haven't been given the right to wash our hands of it, either. We exist for the sake of exhibiting the kingdom of God in hostile territory: "He has showed you, O man, what is good. And what does the Lord require of you? To act justly and to love mercy and to walk humbly with your God" (Mic. 6:8 NIV).

Romans 12:1 teaches that the church's challenge in every generation is to live in the world as a community of "living sacrifices" to God. Since the offering of sacrifices is part of the ritual associated with worship, there is no wonder that Paul would use a word like *latreia* to describe this challenge. Our constant "service" to God and to the watching world is to live out the practical implications of our "worship" to God. "Take your everyday, ordinary life—your sleeping, eating, going-to-work, and walking-around life—and place it before God as an offering" is how *The Message* renders the verse. That's it! We serve God by living out our worship in our everyday, ordinary life events!

Worship as Spiritual Formation

Worship is spiritual formation for the people of God. It teaches us the vocabulary and grammar of the kingdom of God. It slakes the thirst we once tried to satisfy by drinking from the world's poisoned well with the living water of Holy Spirit-presence. It affirms and celebrates the life goals of the kingdom of God—not money, sex, and power, but righteousness, peace, and joy in the Spirit. It offers truth in a world of lies. Love in a world of hatred. It provides healthy relationships in a world of cold indifference.

Quoting Abraham Heschel yet again: "Worship is a way of seeing the world in the light of God."[3] Perhaps Heschel was drawing from his Jewish heritage when he made that insightful observation about the nature of worship. The Hebrew people had been in bondage to their Egyptian overlords. They had been oppressed outsiders. They had been poor and wretched and miserable. Generation after generation, they had been taught the mindset of slave-poverty, slave-identity, and slave-life. Now they were free people at the base of Mount Sinai. But it would take a long time to get the slave mindset out of them. That would be Yahweh's immediate task in their midst through Moses.

So he called Moses onto the mountain (Exod. 19), gave him the Ten Commandments (Exod. 20), detailed a series of laws about how a covenant people should live in community (Exod. 21–24), and offered reams and reams of instruction about building a worship center (Exod. 25–31). Why was the tabernacle so important? Why was that big tent pitched in the middle of the twelve tribes? Why was it illuminated by a pillar of fire at night? Worship would be the center of their life together in community for the next forty years. Eugene Peterson describes the scene around the mountain:

> But Moses was gone a long time, forty days and nights. Meanwhile, the people, impatient to get on with their new life of freedom, decided that they wanted to develop their own worship, worship that, in the phrase of our times, "we can get something out of." So they talked their associate pastor Aaron into providing them worship that satisfied their desire for novelty and excitement, something that turned out to be pretty much a reflection of the gaudy Egyptian world in which they had so recently been oppressed but which they also, as oppressed people often do as excluded outsiders, had lusted after and envied.

> And we know what happened (Exod. 32–33). Their golden calf worship, self-defined and self-serving—refusing to wait, contemptuous of rest, defiant of contemplation—nearly destroyed them. But Moses graciously interceded and started over. He again went up and then came down the mountain (Exod. 34). On his return this time, he put the people to work, preparing them for what was to become the central action of their lives, namely, worship (Exod. 35–40).[4]

They didn't worship 24/7, but their worship defined their new way of reading the world. It didn't pull them away from the desert or family problems or menacing enemies, but it did remind them to deal with all those things by trusting in the Lord. Aaron and his sons, the tent and its furniture, the sacrifices and the songs—all combined to remind the Israelites of their new identity. Not slaves but free. Not bound to Egypt but pilgrims to a Promised Land. Not Pharaoh's but God's. Worship would be their way of seeing their situation in light of God. Why should we not think of its place in our lives the same way?

Or think of the church at the end of the first century. After a period of phenomenal growth, the followers of Jesus Christ began to be persecuted by Roman officials. How could the fledgling, nonmilitaristic community of Christ withstand the awesome power of Rome? Even the last living apostle had not been spared and was in exile on Patmos. But the communication he received from the Lord in that (apparently-but-not-really) God-forsaken place called for believers back on the mainland to let God define their way of reading the world, not Rome. As Rodney Clapp describes it,

> John's vision comes on the Lord's Day—Sunday, the day of worship. Jesus is seen in the liturgical setting of praise and thanksgiving. And he is seen not only as the "firstborn of the dead" but as "the ruler of the kings of the earth" ([Revelation] 1:5). Not only the angels of heaven but the merchants of the earth will

> bow before him (chap. 18). Rather than shy away from politics or commerce, then, John and the communities that embraced his writing celebrated their worship as an indication that the way (or culture) of the Lamb was the final and true way of life.
>
> Despite the fact that they are ragtag, disenfranchised, often persecuted bands of believers, John's communities are bold enough to set their worship head-to-head with the worship of the mighty Roman Empire. Thus two of the seven churches John addresses in his early chapters are in the cities of Smyrna and Pergamum, strongholds of the imperial cult, or worship of the Roman emperor. It is just such churches that John seeks to remind, in and through the mode of liturgy, that things are not as they seem. For all its power and apparent ability to name what is ultimately worthy, Rome's worship is really nothing more than a parody of the praise and service of Israel's God (chaps. 17–18). The real lord and lion turns out to be the Lamb who was led to slaughter (chap. 5); those slain by the beast that is Rome, like the Lamb they follow, are actually conquerors (7:14); those who now seem powerless will receive obeisance from those they fear (3:8–9); and those who suffer poverty are actually rich (2:9).
>
> In short, the business of worship as it is depicted in Revelation is "to stand things on their heads in the perceptions of its audience, to rob the established order of the most fundamental power of all: its sheer facticity."[5]

For the past 1700 years of what this book has dubbed Institutional Church, worship has been stripped of much of its value and power. It has not been so much spiritual formation for the Family of God as an exercise in the marginalization of faith to life. Once the institutional model was imposed on the church of God, church was for Sunday, and real life took place on the other six days of the week. Worship became comfort in a sanctuary rather than focus on truth for the sake of engagement with the tough realities.

Then, during the past few hundred years of modernity, worship became a left-brain exercise in analytic theology. Should prayers be written or spontaneous? Communion open or closed? Sermons expositional or topical? Worship was a self-serving exercise not only in escapism but in celebrating our rightness in doing worship correctly.

More recently, postmodern influences have turned worship into a right-brained phenomenon. Theologians have been relegated to the back seats, while artists have been given the front pews. Worship is now about heart over head. Imagination over explanation. And music has become both the medium and the message. Both modern and postmodern churches have impoverished worship.

Healthy churches will integrate left and right brains to experience whole-person worship. The substantive content of the Christian religion will not be abandoned, yet the acknowledgment of mystery will not be embarrassing. We will speak less of "worship services" than of lives of service for which worship equips us. We will sing and talk and pray less in terms of "I" and "me" and more in terms of "us" and "our." There will be less temptation to a performance mentality on the part of either musicians or teachers for the sake of integrity before the Lord.

Think about it this way: Worship is a way of world-making. It doesn't "take us out of the real world" but instructs us in what the real world is like. God is all in all. Jesus is Alpha and Omega. Spirit-presence is the source of all empowerment for anything that is worthwhile. Instead of being at the edges of life, worship becomes the center. It exalts and celebrates God. It affirms our relationships with one another in God's Family. And it helps us understand how we are to function for his glory on the other days of the week. It both calls to and allows for penitence over our failures from the past. But it mediates grace and pardon and hope for what lies ahead still.

Or, think in terms of a learning process: Worship is a spiritual discipline in which we are formed as kingdom people. From the world, we have learned a culture of preoccupation with ourselves—things and ego. In the church, we are given the chance to unlearn the lies the world has given us. Then, with the rest of the church and for the sake of the world, we relearn what we once glimpsed as little children—that trusting the love of the Heavenly Father is our only real security.

It is time for the so-called "worship wars" to end. So long as they continue, we betray the fact that we just don't get it! Even though we are using new technology and singing new songs, we are still self-absorbed rather than God-intoxicated. When we are determined to show ourselves "distinctive" somehow or, God forbid, "better" and "more like the original church" than someone else, we certainly don't get it! We still have the focus on ourselves rather than on him.

Two Central Truths

When we learn to worship in Spirit and in Truth, we will have learned and modeled two things.

(1) *God is God—and we are not! The unseen reality he knows is so much more authentic and powerful than the things we see that bother us so.*

There is a wonderful little story tucked in the Old Testament that is good to keep in mind on this point. When the Arameans were threatening God's people in the days of Elisha the Prophet, the Lord gave the seer advance warning of certain plots against the King of Israel. When the Aramean king found out there was a holy man with such information, he decided to take care of him. He would find out where he was, send a raiding party, and capture him.

> "Go, find out where he is," the king ordered, "so I can send men and capture him." The report came back: "He is in Dothan."

> Then he sent horses and chariots and a strong force there. They went by night and surrounded the city.
>
> When the servant of the man of God got up and went out early the next morning, an army with horses and chariots had surrounded the city. "Oh, my lord, what shall we do?" the servant asked.
>
> "Don't be afraid," the prophet answered. "Those who are with us are more than those who are with them."
>
> And Elisha prayed, "O Lord, open his eyes so he may see." Then the Lord opened the servant's eyes, and he looked and saw the hills full of horses and chariots of fire all around Elisha. (2 Kings 6:13–17 NIV)

As with Elisha's servant, we are too prone to judge by what we can see. We are too quick to give way to the apparent hopelessness of a situation. We think the enemy of our souls has the upper hand because we can't see the unseen. Worship reminds us that the God of unseen things is behind the scenes for the sake of the triumph of the kingdom of heaven. Lies, death, and evil will not have the last word. Those who are with us are more than those who are with them. God is sovereign over all things.

(2) *Now that we know our relationship to others, we can function as God's servants and instruments in their lives.*

Baptism testifies to us that we are now "in Christ," not the world (Rom. 6:1-11). That we were once dead in trespasses and sins but are now alive by the power of the Holy Spirit in us (Eph. 2:1-10). And the meal that sustains us in this new life is the Lord's Supper, in which we "recognize the body" in each other as we eat and drink together (1 Cor. 11:17-22). We are "one-another people" to all others who know Christ—brothers and sisters in the Family of God.

With these relationships defined in Christ, we understand the language and lifestyle of being missional Christians in the world. Not missionaries, but missional persons. In a word, a *missional* Christian is one who represents Jesus faithfully in the places where he or she is present and has influence. A missional Christian knows how to play well on the road.

Missional Faith: Playing Well on the Road

A missional Christian is a manager or executive who sees her task as representing Jesus to the people she leads; she is a competent professional who does her work with excellence, but her primary self-defined life goal is to bring a taste of the kingdom of God to those with whom she works. He is a salesman who is prompt, enthusiastic, thorough, and ethical, but he is more interested in bearing the image of God faithfully than in getting rich. It is the kindergarten, seventh grade, or graduate school teacher who not only communicates needed information in effective ways but also treats students, fellow-teachers, and maintenance workers with dignity, respect, and love.

Missional Christians don't make points within a church system or within some legalistic interpretation of Scripture for setting up Bible studies or leading people to professions of faith. They are simply being authentic citizens of the kingdom of God. Missional Christians understand that Christ needs someone representing him in every place the members of their church are scattered throughout a community during the week—in offices, at medical clinics, in classrooms, during family outings to the beach, when someone's car has broken down, or after a tragic death in the family three doors down the street.

A believer's task is to learn the thinking and behavior appropriate to his new citizenship. We are *in* the world but are determined not to be *of* the world for Christ's sake. So we assemble, tell the story of our Savior, and participate in community-formation events such as worship, baptism, the Lord's Supper, and one-another fellowship. Yet the assemblies have not been a retreat in a sanctuary but a focus on and preparation for being kingdom people. We leave inspired to be representatives of Christ to everyone with whom we interact—from the traffic cop to the food server to the teenager making change at the grocery store.

As we learn the rhythms of this new way to live, we experience eternal life. Eternal life, after all, is not what we get as a reward for being Christians after we die. It is the new, Spirit-empowered lifestyle that happens among the people of God here and now. The full blossoming of that life awaits the return of Christ, but it has begun already—rooted in a culture of worship and lived out by Christians who understand how to play well on the road.

Chapter Nine

Jesus Could Use a Good PR Agent

"The problem with writing about religion is that you run the risk of offending sincerely religious people, and then they come after you with machetes."
—Dave Barry

"Why is Jesus getting such bad P.R.?" was the headline that caught my eye.[1] The article by Charita Goshay under that title makes about as much sense as anything I've read in a while. Frankly, however, it is more troublesome than comforting to find someone agreeing with me on the point in question.

Goshay begins her piece with a reference to the Hutaree militia. Perhaps you remember how the Hutaree came to light in the spring of 2010, when several people were arrested in Michigan and Indiana. Court documents reported that members of the Michigan-based group had formed a bizarre plot for the mass murder of police officers in hopes of provoking an anti-government revolution across the United States. Dozens of guns and thousands of rounds of ammunition—as well as machetes, swords, gas masks, crack cocaine, and Nazi propaganda documents—were found at the Hutaree camp.

When the story broke, I remember the term "Christian militia"—which some would call an ultimate oxymoron—being used to describe its members. The group's website said the private army was "preparing for the end-time battles to keep the testimony of Jesus Christ alive." From there, Goshay began her reflection.

> Maybe it's because he can't be trademarked, but Jesus is misused a lot these days and for causes that bear little resemblance to his mission.
>
> Does someone who Christians believe walked on water and rose from the dead really need "help" from Midwesterners running around the woods in tiger-stripe fatigues? What kind of deity needs defending anyway?
>
> From Pat Robertson to the Vatican fiasco to the Hutaree, Jesus can't seem to get a break.
>
> Even people who couldn't pick Jesus out in a lineup know better than to believe that the members of the Westboro Baptist Church are representative of the faith.
>
> Giving whole new meaning to "Bible-thumping," the Rev. Fred Phelps and his cult spend virtually all their time, energy and money to inform us that God hates America, soldiers, and gays.[2]

What Ms. Goshay says is what everyone knows. People since the first century have had to form their impressions of Jesus through those of us who claim we know him, follow him, and represent his purposes in the world. And that can be downright scary, a gross misrepresentation of Jesus, and a serious turnoff to people who need to know him.

Is that unfair? Hardly. Writing positively to encourage some Christians who had problems galore in their midst, Paul could nevertheless say this: "Clearly, you are a letter from Christ showing the result of our ministry among you. . . . It is carved not on tablets of stone, but on human hearts" (2 Cor. 3:2–3 NLT). Yet Christians whose actions constitute authentication for a ministry imply the possibility of people whose actions are so ungodly that they bring a ministry into disrepute. Those are the people Ms. Goshay lamented.

Someone who experiences a racist church or homophobic preacher assumes something about Jesus. Another who reads a headline about a "Christian militia group" or an article about clergy making off with church funds may distrust him. And someone who gets close enough to a church to be failed by it or abused by it may curse him.

The Growing Company of "Nones"

Religion simply is not serving the spiritual lives of people very well these days. If you doubt that claim, perhaps you should recall something pointed out already in this book—the fastest growing segment of religious affiliation is neither Catholic, Protestant, Jew, nor Muslim but "None."

A survey conducted by researchers at Trinity College of Hartford, Connecticut, and released in March 2009 generated headlines in practically all the major newspapers in the US. The American Religious Identification Survey (ARIS) has data from 1990, 2001, and—from its most recent use—2008. Although I am no statistician, some of the trends across two decades are probably significant. Interestingly, the title given to the most recent report surely reflects something the researchers themselves considered significant. With surely a pun intended, they labeled it "American Nones: The Profile of the No Religion Population."[3]

The findings in the survey confirmed what most people already suspected. Mainline Protestant groups such as Methodists and Lutherans continue to lose membership. Religious minorities such as Muslims and Mormons grew during the period in question, as did such movements as Wicca and paganism. The "least religious" sections of the country are the Pacific Northwest and Northern New England.

As the title of the report suggests, however, the dramatic finding by the research conducted among more than 54,000 people is how many people are distancing themselves from organized religion in all regions of the United States.

- The only group that grew larger *in every U.S. state* since 2001 was people who opted for the "No Religion" segment of the population.
- The "Nones" constitute 15 percent of American adults—up from 8.1 percent in 1990, growing from 14 to 34 million.
- Twenty-seven percent of respondents said they do not anticipate having a religious service upon their death, and 30 percent of those who were married said their marriage ceremony was not religious.
- The "No Religion" category is significantly larger than the combined total of non-Christian religious groups in the United States.
- Only a small minority of "Nones" say they are atheists.

Do I think this study helps document a trend toward secularism in the United States of America? Yes. But the final item listed above—the fact that only a "small minority" (only seven percent) of persons interviewed said they were atheists—may suggest something else as well. *The disaffection that has created the burgeoning category of "Nones" in America may well reflect the fact that religion is driving people away from God—even people who believe in his existence.*

It may be very revealing, for example, that the largest shift within the category of those who still profess both religious belief and affiliation was from "brand names" such as Roman Catholic, Baptist, or Presbyterian to "generic" cultural or church groups. More specifically, even the number of people who self-identified by the term "Protestant" in previous surveys has declined drastically from approximately seventeen million in 1990 to five million. Meanwhile, the number of people who use nondenominational terms to describe themselves has grown from a rather paltry 194,000 in 1990 to more than eight million.

In commenting on a possible way to interpret this data—and the shift to nondenominational language among Christians in particular—one of the persons who helped supervise the survey ventured a theory. Mark Silk, who directs Trinity College's Program on Public Values, says, "There is now this shift in the non-Catholic population—and maybe among American Christians in general—into a sort of generic, soft evangelicalism."[4]

There seems to be a perspective on all this that has not been taken into account by the ARIS survey and its researchers' analysis. If my hunch is right, maybe "None" or "No Religion" is the self-identification given by some who have dropped out of mainline Christian churches—if not "organized religion" generally—for the simple reason that they see them as too bland, too tame, too unlike their titular founder. In fact, some of these people are looking for anything but a "generic, soft evangelicalism"; they are looking for a challenge to their faith that is worthy of being associated with Jesus Christ.

When Church Is Tame and Bland

Sociologist George Barna has been quite accurate over the past quarter century in taking the pulse of, diagnosing the present situation of, and making predictions about the near-term changes that would be seen in the American church. In 2005, he claimed to have found a large-and-growing population of Christ-confessors who had determined to make Jesus the highest priority of life and to live as his deeply committed followers. Yet these zealous Christians—Barna dubbed them "revolutionaries"—often would not be engaged in traditional church activities. Or, if they still shared fellowship in a local church, they often lived their faith in alternative forms to traditional church programs.

> They have no use for churches that play religious games, whether those games are worship services that drone on without the

> presence of God or ministry programs that bear no spiritual fruit. Revolutionaries eschew ministries that compromise or soft sell our sinful nature to expand organizational turf. They refuse to follow people in ministry leadership positions who cast a personal vision rather than God's, who seek popularity rather than the proclamation of truth in their public statements, or who are more concerned about their own legacy than that of Jesus Christ. They refuse to donate one more dollar to man-made monuments that mark their own achievements and guarantee their place in history. They are unimpressed by accredited degrees and endowed chairs in Christian colleges and seminaries that produce young people incapable of defending the Bible or unwilling to devote their lives to serving others. And Revolutionaries are embarrassed by language that promises Christian love and holiness but turns out to be all sizzle and no substance.[5]

Four areas of life in which Barna saw these revolutionaries as substantially different from church members are these:

- *Passionate for the integration of faith and life.* This typically not only means disciplined reading and study of Scripture but hands-on involvement in serving, sharing their faith, and helping the poor.
- *Committed to biblical truth*. They appreciate basic biblical doctrine but cannot be content to study theology without serious accountability in their spiritual lives, a conscientious pursuit of moral integrity, and the conviction that true faith exhibits itself in obedience to Christ.
- *Focused on the person of Christ.* The highest priority of a revolutionary is conscious and joyous surrender to Jesus Christ; to be a "full-time servant of God" in what Luther would call the priesthood of all believers is their calling.

- *Transformed lives.* Revolutionaries believe the imitation of Christ produces radical, outrageous devotion to God that shows itself in nothing less than a transformed life that experiences love, joy, and peace in the Holy Spirit.

Just as some whose mindsets are thoroughly secular have been turned off by the customary functioning of traditional churches, so have these revolutionary believers been alienated by it. Whether they have come from rigidly traditional Roman Catholic backgrounds, Pentecostal exuberance, or evangelical churches with a strong emphasis on Bible study, they are seeking a challenge more life-consuming, more life-altering than regular assemblies for worship and occasional mountain-peak experiences of summer mission trips or inner-city service projects.

Ironically, both Silk's generic soft evangelicals and Barna's revolutionaries are attracted to Jesus but kept at bay by the church. And it is altogether conceivable to me that some from both groups are counted among the "Nones" of the ARIS survey. As a matter of fact, I know people who consistently identify themselves as "believers, but not terribly interested in church." Or, to use the language those friends taught me through Alcoholics Anonymous, they are "spiritual, but not religious."

The distinction they mean to communicate is the one I recognize as a person who spent forty years of his adult life as the minister of a church. Even as a churchman, man of the cloth, clergy person, or pastor—whatever term you'd use to identify me there—I came to make the same distinction in my own personal life and public ministry. Away from full-time ministry for a while now, it is even more obvious. Maybe I will someday see the distinction as sharply as those in my culture who do not have my deep roots in church life and customs.

It is a wide gulf to bridge for people who started in a more neutral posture than my own—or who have been hurt more seriously by a church betrayal. It is a scab that barely needs to be picked at an AA meeting, however, to get the blood flowing. For that matter, it might be a Bible conference or pastors' meeting.

Sometimes the harm done to a fragile soul—and *all* souls are fragile—early in life and with no sinister intent whatever lingers to drive a wedge between a person and God in her adult life. It is something like the blowout of a deepwater oil well of the sort we watched in the Gulf of Mexico in summer 2010. The rupture took place thousands of feet below the surface; the ugliness of the spill played out in a variety of ways across thousands of square miles. Take Jessi as an illustration of this.

Jessi recently told me of an event that happened to her when she was six—her older sister died. Nineteen now and trying to sort through life to this point in order to take her place in the world as an adult, she realized that a "deepwater blowout" had occurred all those years ago. Can six-year-old children understand traumatic death? Can they process answers that cause adults to struggle? Can they reorient themselves easily and naturally? Of course not. But some of the things she heard (e.g., "Honey, this is just God's will" or "Jesus took your sister to be with him") and at least one visual image that lingers with her have made faith difficult for Jessi in her teen years. "I was confused about what was happening and was looking for somebody to help me beyond what my grieving, struggling family had been able to explain," she said. "I can still to this day see myself sitting alone in the pew. I think I was waiting for someone to come to me, to help me, to nurture me and help me understand."

You and I can look back at that scene and explain it away. Nobody meant any harm. There was nothing that anyone could have said. Her level of maturity put so many things beyond her. Yes. Yes! *Yes!* All those things are true. Yet they don't address the situation now the way an arm, lap, or shoulder could have on that day. Our "theologies of pain" may be sophisticated and surely have value in a variety of settings; a "Jesus presence" to weep beside Lazarus' tomb or to sit silently with a suffering human being will almost always be worth more.

Rediscovering Jesus

With the numbers showing both a decline in church membership and in church attendance, countless projects have been launched to "get people back to church." If the goal is to get people to reconnect with what most of them identify as church, the next thousand of these efforts will be no more successful than the failed last ten thousand of them.

Too many people have already settled the issue of church. They're done with it. Over it. Out of there. And they aren't interested in re-thinking, re-entering, or even re-inventing it. But you just might get their attention with this radical, engaging, challenging, life-transforming, healing, rescuing person named Jesus of Nazareth. In fact, I think it is the only hope we have for communicating with a postmodern world. The best argument is not a syllogism or well-written book but a *living demonstration of kindness and acceptance, grace made incarnate, or love emptying itself for the sake of others.*

What I have in mind is something very different from a phone number to call and an address to visit next Sunday. It is somebody daring—perhaps even several somebodies joining together—to reach out to a Muslim family whose breadwinner was injured or has died, a street person who needs a friend, or an angry unbeliever who delights in making him (or them) flinch with vocabulary that ranges from salty to sordid. People who will never rethink church will rethink their image of Jesus if someone engages them lovingly as a servant of Jesus—without claiming the right to cram Jesus down their throats.

Syndicated columnist Leonard Pitts dared to risk outrage on the part of his readers by reporting the ARIS information cited above in an opinion piece he entitled "Religion is driving people away from God." Here is his explanation for the increased alienation from the church:

> Religion has become an ugly thing. People of faith usually respond to that ugliness—by which I mean a seemingly endless

> cycle of scandal, controversy, hypocrisy, violence and TV preachers saying idiotic things—in one of two ways. Either they defend it—making them part of the problem—or they regard it as a series of isolated, albeit unfortunate, episodes. But irreligious people do neither.[6]

He is correct. Religion *can be*—and sometimes is—an ugly thing. As a passionate and practicing Christian, I yield the point. I am embarrassed over it. I apologize for my contributions to the church's ugliness, and I ask God to forgive me of any contribution I have made to putting obstacles on some soul's would-be path to Jesus.

I take no comfort in the fact that this is not a new problem. The Hebrew prophets long ago lamented that people were putting their religious rituals in the place of integrity and offering donations to worthy causes as their substitute for showing compassion to their neighbors. In the eighth century before the birth of Jesus, one of those prophets minced no words about it:

> I hate, I despise your festivals,
> and I take no delight in your solemn assemblies.
> Even though you offer me your burnt-offerings and grain-offerings,
> I will not accept them;
> and the offerings of well-being of your fatted animals
> I will not look upon.
> Take away from me the noise of your songs;
> I will not listen to the melody of your harps. (Amos 5:21–23)

The very things that had been commanded in Jewish Law—worship, offerings, gifts, songs, and the other trappings of religion—were now being denounced by a Spirit-guided prophet of Yahweh. What was going on? The people had learned to play the religious game of the Corleone family in *The Godfather* movies. So long as they were "in church" and "connected" and "donating," their lives could be corrupt and their hearts hard. Even for those of us who do not play the game in quite so radical a fashion as Michael Corleone, our churchgoing can still smack of a game. And it interferes with the line of sight someone otherwise could have to see God.

The alternative that eighth-century BC prophet set before his people was certainly open to criticism for its naïve simplicity.

> But let justice roll down like waters,
> and righteousness like an ever-flowing stream. (Amos 5:24)

"Naïve simplicity" indeed! The *justice* Amos pleaded for was not a reform of the police and the courts that meted out retribution to criminals (i.e., *retributive* justice); it is what we would call *distributive* justice—compassion for and care given to the weakest and most helpless in the land. The *righteousness* he longed to see was not faithfulness to a list of moral demands but the covenantal uprightness one lives before God; it is honoring God by living into his purpose for you as his image-bearer. A good commentary on Amos 5:24 is provided by his counterpart in the New Testament. At James 1:27, the half-brother of Jesus wrote: "Religion that is pure and undefiled before God, the Father, is this: to care for orphans and widows in their distress, and to keep oneself unstained by the world."

Whether spoken of by Amos or James, or described in the Old or New Testament, the essential elements of pure and undefiled religion remain the same: *holiness* and *compassion*. One must live with God-first focus that reveals itself in grace and compassion toward others. Isaiah agreed with Amos (see Isa. 1:10 ff); Jesus affirmed them both (see Matt. 22:37–40); and John repeated it for good measure (see 1 John 4:20–21). And while Isaiah predicted it, Jesus established it, and John was part of it, their message was not "church." It was love for God that plays out as love for people. That is what people saw about Jesus that they miss seeing in so much of the church's activity.

Positive PR for Jesus

Ah, but when somebody does get it right, you can't help noticing. It makes all the difference somewhere, for someone. And people think about Jesus. No, they *see* Jesus. They are drawn to him and inspired to be like him. In her article that laments all the bad PR Jesus gets, Ms. Goshay winds up by telling the beautiful story of Sam LaBarba. Sam wasn't the mayor or police chief or bishop of his church. He was a humble man in bad health who was deeply involved in helping immigrants and ex-convicts find their way in a new, strange environment. When he died, a community of believers knew they had lost an effective PR agent for Jesus. So the newspaper testimony continues:

> A parishioner at St. Anthony Catholic Church in Canton, Ohio, [Sam] was deeply involved in its efforts to assist Hispanics who were moving into the community, and was co-founder of Let's Talk, an outreach for ex-offenders to help them restart their lives.
>
> Sam . . . once told me that his immigrant parents taught him that everyone was equal. To his last days, he went as far as his wheelchair would take him to preach the gospel in ways that made Jesus' words more than just talk.[7]

Fortunately, the sometimes-imperious church is filled with warm, hospitable, loving people who break down the barrier between those who have been alienated from church but who desperately need a link to Christ. Martin's experience, for example, responds to Jessi's that was described earlier.

Martin was a preacher's son who had seen too much that was too disappointing about church. By his mid-teens, he was jaded and distant. It was easy for him to speak of hypocrisy and phoniness. He used just those descriptors to defend his own determination to have nothing to do with church. Then he was involved in a grinding automobile accident that happened because of the alcohol he had been drinking. The very people he had rejected as hypocrites and pretenders stood by his family, showed incredible concern for him, and refused to judge and blame him with the sort of severity he judged and blamed himself. Some of them even told their own stories of alcohol or drugs or jail.

"Before all that happened, I thought I hated 'religion' and 'the church,'" he says now. "After seeing how real Christianity worked through those marvelous people I had judged so mercilessly, I gained a whole new outlook on things." When I met Martin and learned his story, he was a student in a religious studies class I was teaching; his life is committed to Christian ministry. He will tell you in a heartbeat that his intention in ministry is not to maintain the institution our society knows as church but to find creative ways to reach people with the incarnate love of Christ that touched him. I think it is safe to say that the driving question of his ministry will not be "What does church polity dictate here?" but "How would Jesus respond here?"

To the degree that you can turn Jesus' words into "more than just talk" today, you are providing the sort of priceless PR he has been lacking of late. You will be showing people the Jesus who walked around in Judea, Samaria, and Galilee before we obscured his image with our militias, homophobes, and heretics. You may even see some of the barriers fall and an occasional heart open itself to him.

Chapter Ten

CHURCH AS DEFENDER OF HUMAN DIGNITY

"I belong to a church
that throws birthday parties
for whores at 3:30 in the morning."
—TONY CAMPOLO

Tony Campolo is quite a character. He is a sociologist. He is a counselor. He is a preacher. And he is a troubler of complacent consciences. A case in point is the story he tells in his book *The Kingdom of God Is a Party*.[1] The story is about a late-night experience he had in Hawaii several years ago. In the wee hours of the morning, he was looking for a place to get a bite to eat. He wound up in a place that, in his own words, deserved the old epithet of "greasy spoon." He sat down on a stool at a counter and ordered a cup of coffee and a donut. Gulping them down so he could get out of a place where he felt pretty uncomfortable, the front door of the diner swung open and in walked eight or nine loud and outrageously dressed prostitutes.

Several of them plopped down at the same counter where he was sitting and talked back and forth in pretty crude, as well as loud, language. He decided it was time to beat a hasty retreat from a place where a Christian had no business being. Then he overheard the woman sitting immediately beside him say, "Tomorrow's my birthday. I'm going to be thirty-nine."

One of the women in her company of friends replied to her in what Campolo said was a nasty tone to dismiss the whole thing. "So what do you want from me?" the woman bellowed. "A birthday party? You want me to get you a cake and sing 'Happy Birthday'?"

"Come on," replied the woman sitting next to Campolo. "Why do you have to be so mean? I was just telling you, that's all. Why do you have to put me down? I was just telling you it was my birthday. I don't want anything from you. I mean, why should you give me a birthday party? I've never had a birthday party in my whole life. Why should I have one now?"

If you know anything about Campolo and his fabled exploits, you won't be surprised at what happened next. Instead of leaving, he endured the noise and smoke and language until the women left. Then he asked the fellow behind the counter if those "ladies of the evening" were regulars at his place. Specifically, he asked about the woman who had been sitting next to him. "Yeah!" he said. "That's Agnes. Yeah, she comes in here every night. Why d'ya wanta know?" And Campolo told the fellow he would like to throw a birthday party for her the following day.

The man thought about it, grinned, and said, "That's great! I like it! That's a great idea!" So he turned around and called his wife out from the kitchen, where she was doing the cooking. "Hey! Come out here!" he said to her. "This guy's got a great idea. Tomorrow's Agnes' birthday. This guy wants us to go in with him and throw a birthday party for her—right here—tomorrow night!" And the woman said that was a wonderful idea—that nobody ever did anything kind for Agnes. So they made a plan. Campolo would come back the next morning at 2:30 with decorations and a cake and help fix up the place for Agnes' party. The couple running the diner agreed—with the stipulation that *they* would provide the cake.

Sure enough, Campolo was back the next morning with some crepe-paper decorations he had found. And he had made a sign out of a big piece of cardboard that read "Happy Birthday, Agnes!" The decorations were hung. And by a little after 3:00 a.m. in the little diner, it was crowded with prostitutes—for the cook had spread the word about a party for Agnes. A man and his wife, a preacher, and wall-to-wall prostitutes!

Agnes walked through the door at almost exactly 3:30, and everybody screamed "Happy Birthday!" She was stunned. Her mouth fell open. One of the women with her steadied her, as her knees seemed to wobble a bit. And the singing began: "Happy birthday, dear Agnes, happy birthday to you." As the singing died out and the cake with candles blazing came through the door from the kitchen, Agnes burst into tears. She just lost it. A prostitute was having her first-ever birthday party!

As people pressed her to cut the cake, she said to Harry—the name of the fellow who ran the place—in a very soft voice, "Look, Harry, is it all right with you if I . . . I mean is it okay if I kind of . . . what I want to ask you is . . . is it okay if I keep the cake a little while? I mean, is it all right if we don't eat it right away?" Harry allowed that the cake was hers and she could do anything with it she wanted. "Sure! It's okay. If you want to keep the cake, keep the cake," he said. "Take it home, if you want to."

"Can I?" she asked. Looking then at Campolo, she said, "I live just down the street a couple of doors. I want to take the cake home, OK? I'll be right back. Honest!" Campolo writes:

> She got off the stool, picked up the cake, and carrying it like it was the Holy Grail, walked slowly toward the door. As we all just stood there motionless, she left.
>
> When the door closed, there was a stunned silence in the place. Not knowing what else to do, I broke the silence by saying, "What do you say we pray?"
>
> Looking back on it now, it seems more than strange for a sociologist to be leading a prayer meeting with a bunch of prostitutes in a diner in Honolulu at 3:30 in the morning. But then it just felt like the right thing to do. I prayed for Agnes. I prayed

for her salvation. I prayed that her life would be changed and that God would be good to her.

When I finished, Harry leaned over the counter and with a trace of hostility in his voice, he said, "Hey! You never told me you were a preacher. What kind of church do you belong to?" In one of those moments when just the right words came, I answered, "I belong to a church that throws birthday parties for whores at 3:30 in the morning."

Harry waited a moment and then almost sneered as he answered, "No you don't. There's no church like that. If there was, I'd join it. I'd join a church like that!"[2]

The Gospel and Human Dignity

The gospel of Jesus Christ affirms, defends, and enhances human dignity. The message of salvation is about restoring the relationship not only between God and humankind but also among divided and alienated human beings. The wedge that 1700 years of institutional Christianity has driven between insiders and outsiders, males and females, one racial or ethnic group and another, wealthy and poor, one social class and another, prostitutes and preachers is contrary to the explicit will of God on the pages of Holy Scripture. All of us know that. But we haven't lived into it very well.

The vision of the kingdom of God Jesus taught and modeled does not allow discrimination based on race or class or wealth. That vision was unique to Jesus and his early followers—an ever-so-brief reversal of accepted and institutionalized divisions in the human race.

The ancient Greeks and Romans are sometimes hailed for their noble sense of democracy. The fact is that "democracy" had a very specific definition in Athens, Rome, and throughout the ancient world in general. For example, the Athenian democracy included a tiny minority of that city-state's population—landowning adult males. Their wives and children were property. Their slaves—well over half the total population—had no rights whatever. And all non-Greeks were "barbarians" by definition. The Romans inherited and perpetuated the same model. So did the Constitution of the United States of America. Women could not vote or hold office. Children had few legal rights or protections. And Africans brought to America as slaves were not counted as human.

The Old Testament is quite remarkable for the high view of humankind it reflects. All human beings are made in the image of God and bear likeness to him (Gen. 1:26; see Ps. 8:4–8). Because Judaism was a regulation of behavior within an existing social order rather than the inauguration of the Messianic Kingdom, however, its Scripture still reflects class divisions and distinctions. Israel is the people of God, and other nations are "foreigners." Free persons and slaves are distinguished in terms of their rights. And there are clear distinctions between male and female. Granted that, foreigners, slaves, and females had rights and protections under the Law of Moses that they did not enjoy in neighboring cultures. Charles Tabor explains:

> Jesus alone among all religious founders and leaders rejected all forms of discrimination and insisted that all human beings ought to be treated in exactly the same way. His own dealings with women, with children, with lepers and other ritually polluted people, and with foreigners radically undermined all the distinctions that human societies of his day unanimously institutionalized. He extended the category "neighbor" to all humankind and insisted that the two Great Commandments applied to all; and he taught his disciples to love even their enemies. These surely were among the reasons why Jesus' peers found him troublingly subversive and therefore condemned him.
>
> The apostles, and especially Paul, picked up and taught the same thing (note that in Galatians 3:28 Paul, following Jesus,

> specifically and categorically rejected the three Old Testament grounds for discrimination [i.e., Israelites and foreigners, male and female, slave and free] in the church), though the church never actually practiced this teaching as radically as it might have. . . . The power of prevalent custom in Jewish and Greco-Roman societies prevented the early church from practicing fully what its own teaching taught it to do.[3]

The early church began the pursuit of Jesus' vision of the kingdom of God and affirmed human dignity in a way unique to its time. Much of its impact and effectiveness in evangelism surely traces to the fact that marginalized persons were included in its life. Thus the scholars of religion at Jerusalem initially were inclined to dismiss the whole phenomenon of Christianity because its leaders were "unschooled, ordinary men" (Acts 4:13). The same was true in the larger Roman Empire. Paul mentioned that the church of God at Corinth had a minimum of wealthy, educated, and powerful members (1 Cor. 1:26). Part of the scandal of the cross that kept some of the rich and powerful at a distance was unquestionably its elimination of class and privilege barriers.

One of the most interesting of Paul's letters—although it is the shortest of them—is his Epistle to Philemon. Written from Rome during Paul's first imprisonment there, it reflects a personal ethical dilemma the apostle faced. One of the people Paul contacted during his house arrest and helped either convert or disciple was Onesimus. Onesimus was a runaway slave who had made his way to Rome. Now, consistent with his status as a Christian, he was trying to make restitution for any harm he had caused others. Somehow, in the course of their many conversations, it dawned on Paul that he knew Onesimus' former owner-master!

Thus Paul faced the challenge of encouraging Onesimus to return property and money he had stolen from Philemon—including his own person—and leading the Christian Philemon to act in a way more

Christlike than merely as a legal owner in hearing his slave's confession of sin and receiving the restitution he was prepared to offer. One doesn't have to be creative at all to read between the lines of what Paul proposes:

> While here in jail, I've fathered a child, so to speak. And here he is, hand-carrying this letter—Onesimus! He was useless to you before; now he's useful to both of us. I'm sending him back to you, but it feels like I'm cutting off my right arm in doing so. I wanted in the worst way to keep him here as your stand-in to help out while I'm in jail for the Message. But I didn't want to do anything behind your back, make you do a good deed that you hadn't willingly agreed to.
>
> Maybe it's all for the best that you lost him for a while. You're getting him back now for good—and no mere slave this time, but a true Christian brother! That's what he was to me—he'll be even more than that to you.
>
> So if you still consider me a comrade-in-arms, welcome him back as you would me. If he damaged anything or owes you anything, chalk it up to my account. This is my personal signature—Paul—and I stand behind it. (I don't need to remind you, do I, that you owe your very life to me?) Do me this big favor, friend. You'll be doing it for Christ, but it will also do my heart good.
>
> I know you well enough to know you will. You'll probably go far beyond what I've written. (Philem. 10–21 MSG)

The doctrine of the fundamental dignity of every human being is indivisible from the gospel itself. As one theologian puts it: "[I]t is through Jesus that we are summoned to become more truly human, to reflect the image of God into the world."[4] Yet human dignity or the call to be more truly human is not a "doctrine" so much as it is a lived reality that is either present in or absent from any community of people that offers itself as Christ's church. And when the church took the organizational structure of empire in the fourth century, it quickly retreated from being a (supernatural, Spirit-created) community of racial, gender, and social equals to reflect the (natural, unspiritual) dominant cultural model of discrimination and exclusion. The post-Constantine church stood this Pauline text on its head: "So we have stopped evaluating others by what the world thinks about them. Once I mistakenly thought of Christ that way, as though he were merely a human being. How differently I think about him now! What this means is that those who become Christians become new persons. They are not the same anymore, for the old life is gone. A new life has begun!" (2 Cor. 5:16–17 NLT).

If you have ever wondered how oppression ranging from medieval servitude in "Christian Europe" to pre-Civil War slavery in "God-fearing America" to contemporary racism and on-demand abortion in "red-state enclaves of traditional family values" could survive, the answer is not that difficult. It is only Jesus' radical view of human dignity carried by the gospel that undermines our natural (i.e., fallen) willingness to view people as worthwhile if and only if they are pretty or wealthy, powerful or smart, healthy or influential. Lacking Christ's eyes through which to see others, we judge one another by these worldly standards. But looking at everyone through his eyes changes things. And the Old Church of division, caste, and discrimination becomes the New Church, a place where part of the salvation process for every person is the discovery of his or her essential dignity as a person bearing God's own image. As N. T. Wright wrote:

> The life of believers, individually and collectively, is intended to incarnate the biblical reality of human dignity. The church is called to be an alternative society, living in a contrasting style in the midst of the world. Its members are, in God's design, not self-promoting, as the world is; they are not competitive, as the world is; they do not advance at the expense of others, as the world does; they do not take advantage of the weakness of others, as

the world does. They love one another and do good to and for one another. Failing that, there is no compelling reason for the world to pay attention. Which is to say that the only means by which Christians can commend a truly godly vision of human rights is to incarnate them in their individual and collective lives, to announce God's actions and intentions that constitute the Gospel, and to act justly in the name of God.[5]

Receiving Truth "in Context"

People can apprehend truth only in a cultural context. That is why churches or ministries that send out missionaries insist that those men and women study the new culture and find ways to connect the gospel to it with language, metaphors, and stories that mean something to its people. By virtue of its divine origin, the gospel message is transcultural (or, perhaps better, *supra*-cultural) but still must be presented in the vocabulary of place and time.

The language of our own culture has changed radically in recent times. To use the language of Charles Kraft, we are all as immersed in our cultures as fish are in water. It is the medium within which we move and are forced to function. If we are going to speak the gospel faithfully in this generation, we must give some serious thought to the fact that language, methods, and communication techniques may need to be different than the ones that reached us. We will have to be as responsible to the cross-cultural nature of communication within our highly-developed, information-based, urbanized settings as missionaries are when going to nonliterate, nomadic, and rural peoples. So let's get clear about the message and the matter of best practices for its delivery.

What is our message? That Jesus has died, been buried, and risen again according to the Scriptures to bring us to God. This is the gospel, as summarized by Paul at 1 Corinthians 15:1 ff. That different people react to this heaven-revealed, Spirit-empowered message differently based on their cultures is illustrated from that apostle's same epistle to the church at Corinth.

> For the message about the cross is foolishness to those who are perishing, but to us who are being saved it is the power of God. For it is written, "I will destroy the wisdom of the wise, and the discernment of the discerning I will thwart." Where is the one who is wise? Where is the scribe? Where is the debater of this age? Has not God made foolish the wisdom of the world? For since, in the wisdom of God, the world did not know God through wisdom, God decided, through the foolishness of our proclamation, to save those who believe. For Jews demand signs and Greeks desire wisdom, but we proclaim Christ crucified, a stumbling block to Jews and foolishness to Gentiles, but to those who are the called, both Jews and Greeks, Christ the power of God and the wisdom of God. For God's foolishness is wiser than human wisdom, and God's weakness is stronger than human strength. (1 Cor. 1:18–25)

This text displays Paul's acute awareness that the Jewish and Greco-Roman cultures of his day were quite different. He understood that their reactions to Christ reflected that difference. So he took those reactions into account in approaching them with his missionary message.[6]

Paul, a freeborn Roman citizen of Jewish extraction, was uniquely able to be a missionary to both cultures. So he worked from his personal background to connect with Jews as a Jew and with Gentiles as a Gentile. But his goal was always to preach Christ so as to break down the barrier between Jew and Gentile. He believed that one of the effects of the gospel was the creation of "one new humanity" (Eph. 2:15) out of once-alienated races and cultures.

With the dual understandings that different cultures require different approaches with the gospel but that all cultures are intended eventually to give way to a single new identity in Christ, what does all this mean to our place in history? Specifically, what does it mean about preaching the cross? The culture of the past few centuries has changed the world forever. Nothing will take us back to the pre-Renaissance, pre-Enlightenment, pre-Reformation world. The turning of that corner in history empowered individuals against despotic governments and oppressive religion. Western civilization became a science-guided, science-adoring culture. The battle cry became this: *Enough focused brainpower will solve all our problems!* So we created laboratories and hospitals, big universities and multinational corporations, democracy and capitalism, nonconformist individualism in ethics, and radical autonomy in religion.

While the mindset of modernity has been productive and irreversible, taking that worldview to its most extreme forms has been highly problematic. We became so reductionist in philosophy and religion that we made the physical sciences our sole guide to truth. We became so materialistic in lifestyle that drug use, sexual license, and money defined the good life. We became so arrogant in social and political life and European-American white males so dictated life in general that racism, sexism, ethnocentrism, and other forms of might-makes-right idolatry were threatening to destroy the world. The very scientific establishment that made the means to it now told us that we were only seconds to minutes away from the midnight of nuclear self-destruction.

During that time of radical modernity, the gospel survived. Christian evangelists, scholars, and universities used the tools of science to argue for the historical, archaeological, and geographic accuracy of Scripture. True to the time and its demand for certitude, we engaged the "battle for inerrancy." Denominations and local churches looked and functioned very much like corporations and small businesses. Mission was undertaken to people groups rather than individuals because of the capitalist model of dollars-per-soul approaches to evangelism. Churches became essentially passive in missions—functioning very much as a group of investor-stockholders looking for a good return on capital outlay. It was the water in which we were swimming. It was the cultural context. But the modernist mindset—which we were obliged to be discerning enough to engage—eventually became the mindset of the Body of Christ and compromised its integrity.

The Dawn of Anti-modernity

Now the full dawn of Postmodernity—maybe we should just call it *Anti-modernity*—has come. It has its own problems and shortcomings. Every cultural shift does! Although some people have opted to make it an easy target for wholesale condemnation, it is the water in which this generation swims. It is the mood of the university. It is the milieu in which our peers—especially the under-thirty-five crowd—work and play, read books and watch TV, go to the movies and relate to friends.

I have suggested more than once that perhaps this cultural shift should be called *Anti*-modernity for the simple reason that Postmodernity is less a series of systematic beliefs as it is a reaction against the Modern Era and its penchant for rational certainties, hierarchies of power, and minimization of human dignity—whether by science or government, by business or religion. And it certainly has features that are appropriate as vehicles for communicating the gospel of Christ—so long as we don't swallow the whole menu and compromise the message, as we sometimes did with Modernity.

For example, there are still some prominent scientists whose commitment to Modernity's worship of the physical sciences has them affirming that human reason uncovers by its unaided power all that is worth knowing, anything that can be called "true." The late Carl Sagan was a paradigm modernist. He still has heirs in men such as Richard Dawkins, Stephen J. Gould, Christopher Hitchens, and Stephen Hawking. Their claim is that religion is a delusion held over from a superstitious, ignorant past and that ethics and metaphysical issues are quite literally non-sensical because they are not subject to scientific formulae. But there are also physicists such as John Polkinghorne or Francis Collins. They comment on the limits as well as powers of science; they see reasons for worship in the fields of their expertise.

During an interview for the Public Broadcasting Service, Dr. Collins made the sort of statement that reflects a faith that can and will thrive in the postmodern world. Asked by the interviewer to describe his faith, he didn't point to traditional theistic arguments or claim mathematical certitude about his conclusions. He used the sort of incarnational theology that one hears so commonly among postmodern men and women. "I guess I'd call myself a serious Christian," he began. "That is someone who believes in the reality of Christ's death and resurrection, and who tries to integrate that into daily life and not just relegate it to something you talk about on Sunday morning."[7]

"Incarnational theology" is God-talk (i.e., theology) personified (i.e., made real, put in human form). In its original and purest form, incarnational theology is this: "The Word became flesh and lived among us, and we have seen his glory, the glory as of a father's only son, full of grace and truth" (John 1:14). In its secondary and blemished corporate form, it is the church: "The church is Christ's body, in which he speaks and acts, by which he fills everything with his presence" (Eph. 1:23b MSG). In its secondary and blemished personal forms, it is you and me: "I have been crucified with Christ; and it is no longer I who live, but it is Christ who lives in me. And the life I now live in the flesh I live by faith in the Son of God, who loved me and gave himself for me" (Gal. 2:19b–20).

For more and more people in our world, truth is not the final line of a syllogism. It is not something found through formal argument. Truth is something engaging, real, and life-changing that links me with other spiritual explorers in a meaningful way. And this view of truth invites us to tell people about Jesus of Nazareth! He is truth enfleshed. He is the Way, the Truth, and the Life—who changes one and all who follow him as apprentices and simultaneously links all his followers to one another as well.

Postmoderns like the convenience and ease of communication through cell phone, Internet, and text messaging. They form social networks using popular Web sites. But they also like the real presence of warm-bodied human beings for conversation and sharing. They dislike "religion"—which they associate with Modernity's formulas, power structures, and abuse of persons—but are in search of authentic "spirituality." They like the pre-Christendom Jesus who loved, healed, and empowered people, but they don't have much use for the post-Constantinean Jesus of organized religiosity.

Were you startled at the great numbers of young people in Vatican Square or gathered in other places around the world during Pope John Paul II's final hours? It was because of his potential as a transitional role in the Roman Catholic Church. As the head of a modern institution whose rituals, creeds, structures, and treatment of persons have driven away many, his warm, good-humored, self-effacing, in-touch-with-people manner had been a welcome change for Roman Catholics. His strong leadership on behalf of freedom in Europe and social justice around the world made him heroic in his frailty. He confessed his church's failures during the terrible time of the Holocaust. He spoke out for peace and against economic exploitation. Therefore, he was seen as a spiritual force by many who had left the Roman Catholic Church—or had repudiated religion in general. He was a missionary to a changed church culture. His successor, Pope Benedict XVI, has not generated such passion. To the contrary, his stiff manner and stern pronouncements have caused many who thought they saw hope in Rome to turn away in despair.

The single perfect exemplar of spirituality is Jesus of Nazareth. He was no mystic in the mountains or guru protected from ordinary people living real life. He went to dinner parties and weddings. He told stories about such routine things as sweeping a house, planting seed, tending animals, and fishing—all of which he seemed not only to know about but also to have experienced. He talked with people as they walked and ate and rested together. He cooked breakfast for his friends. He cried at funerals. He sweated. He got bellyaches and tired feet. He laughed. He got mad. In other words, Jesus was not raising the subject of God for discussion. He wasn't presenting a plan for influencing a God who lives at a distance. He was God in the flesh and God in the lives of people—intimately involved in this world. He was God who cares so much about us that he would die before giving up hope for us. And it is living in the shadow of the cross of Jesus that makes his story believable and engaging and life-transforming to people you can influence.

As anti-modernity, postmodernity decries cold intellectualism, resents the abuse of power, and identifies with the weak and marginalized. Why, that sounds a lot like Jesus. The pre-Christian Jesus! He chided the Pharisees for thinking they would find eternal life in their scholarly disputes over Scripture. He was on the receiving end of the abuse of power. He was marginalized and excluded himself as a poor Jewish peasant under the Roman boot and finally put to death as an anti-establishment agitator. Once you meet God at Calvary in the person of the crucified Jesus, you will know that God has been among us. And you will know that you can live in relationship with him as a child of God forever.

Back to the Church Harry Would Join

One who follows Christ and whose heart and life are in transformation by the Spirit of God displays ever-increasing concern for people who are hungry or homeless, drug-addicted or imprisoned. He or she understands that serving them is a way to serve Christ (see Matt. 25:31 ff). That's why Christians tend to be the best pool of volunteers for helping schools, working for the American Heart Association, or sending relief supplies to hurricane victims. It is why so many church and parachurch ministries shower compassion on the Agneses of the world.

These are all efforts to affirm—or, in some instances, to reclaim—human dignity. A faithful church must follow Jesus to live the gospel in its totality by both proclaiming and enfleshing God's love. By sacrificing in order to serve those who have been beaten up and left beside the road to die. For the teeming millions who think their lives don't count and that they are nobodies, the church is in the world to say, "You matter to the God who knows your name—and who sent us to find you."

Put another way, don't we all feel like Harry? Wouldn't we all like to be part of a church that throws birthday parties for prostitutes at 3:30 in the morning? That's just the kind of church Jesus died and rose from the dead to create.

Chapter Eleven

The Ministry of Amateurs

"Let us enter the new week
ready to minister in our homes,
our neighborhoods, our schools,
and our places of work."
—Closing Lord's Day charge to members of Brunswick Church

Most people know that the earliest Christian church modeled its life after the Jewish synagogue. Although there was structure to the synagogue, there was nothing that would strike an observer as essentially hierarchical or sacramental in its nature. A synagogue had "officers,"[1] to be sure (see Luke 4:20). But they were basically respected older men who called the Abrahamic people of a given city or locale together to affirm the identity of the group, brokered that congregation's activity to the larger community, and performed occasional duties related to the community. Synagogue worship reflected its nonsacerdotal nature. That is, it functioned through the activity of persons who were neither priests nor clerics in the generally understood meaning of those terms. What our culture would term "clergy" (i.e., Levitical priests) officiated at the temple, but "laity" (i.e., designated persons from any tribe in Israel) were visible and functional in the synagogue.

For example, a typical worship assembly consisted of the word—both read and sung—and prayer. Israel's God was praised with the familiar songs of the Psalter. Prayers were offered. Expositions were brought from the biblical text. There was enough informality about the synagogue that any male member of the local community could be asked to read the Holy Scripture and exhort hearers to piety and devotion. And it was not even unusual for visitors to be invited to make comments on what was read. Thus Jesus was the reader for the passage from the Prophets—always read after a section of Torah—in a synagogue service at Nazareth (Luke 4:16-21). The missionary Paul routinely used the synagogue as a starting place for teaching about Jesus in various cities he visited because of its custom of asking visiting male Israelites to speak (Acts 13:15).

This pattern of praise, exhortation from the Word of God, and prayer seems to have been the one followed not only by those first Jewish churches in and around Jerusalem but among Gentile congregations that formed much later. In reading Paul's letter to Corinth, for example, there are issues related to worship. It seems that the very simplicity of Christian worship made it susceptible to abuse in certain situations. So the apostle gave guidelines designed less to formalize the church's assemblies than to keep them from becoming utterly chaotic (see 1 Cor. 14:27–36). What is interesting to note here is that anyone in attendance at one of those assemblies was a potential presenter. Thus Paul prefaces his broad rules of order with this observation: "What then shall we say, brothers? When you come together, everyone has a hymn, or a word of instruction, a revelation, a tongue or an interpretation. All of these must be done for the strengthening of the church" (1 Cor. 14:26 NIV).

Professionalizing the Church

In the Constantinean Revolution of the fourth century, the pattern of leadership by believers other than "ordained priests"—both in formal worship settings and daily ministry—changed dramatically and decisively. It is in form and vocabulary after this date that notions of a privileged clergy or ordained priesthood emerges. Participants would soon become mere observers, and active engagement in ministry would give way to support for persons whose profession was ministry.

After Constantine, the worship and life of the Christian church moved away from the synagogue model very quickly to parallel the temple precedent of priest, sacrifice, and observers. The Lord's Supper as a meal of communion and thanksgiving became a re-sacrificing of the body of Christ; the table of communion became an altar. But if there is now a sacrifice to be placed on an altar, there must be a priest. Just anyone can give thanks at a meal or join in a communion, but not "just anyone" can lay a sacrifice on a holy altar. So the next several centuries saw functions become offices and witnessed a distinct hierarchy emerge in the church. "Clergy" officiated at communion and baptism; "laity" observed in silence—except to respond as told. What was true of worship in particular was reflected in all other aspects of the life of the church.

A doctrine evolved over the decades following Constantine that the church is the saving institution. Rites such as baptism and the Lord's Supper soon became sacraments. So did marrying and burying people. And the sacraments became the province of the church—in particular the "ordained" priests who dispensed them. People were granted or denied access to the institution and the sacraments through the mediation of a human priesthood. Power of that sort was immense and heady—and led to abuses of the worst sort. The church became the dispenser of salvation. The beautiful New Testament notion of the church as the Body of Christ to which all the saved are added by the Lord Jesus became the abusive doctrine that there is no salvation available to needy sinners except through the ministrations of the institutional church. To offend the clergy was to be cut off from salvation. To die in certain situations meant burial in unsanctified soil. To bribe or otherwise curry favor with church officials was to be assured of salvation while in league with Satan himself as a criminal or heretic.

When the Reformation Movement of the sixteenth century protested many of the departures that had taken place between the first three centuries and Luther's famous ninety-five theses, one of the emphatic doctrines that emerged was *the priesthood of all believers*. But the "doctrine" never quite returned to the earliest practice of the Christians. The caste system of clergy and laity has continued to dominate the Christian religion in practically all its forms. The idea that the church is the saving institution that grants or denies access to God persists. Most people have made peace with some sort of clergy-laity distinction. We designate the "upper class" by honorific titles such as "Pastor Sam" or "Dr. Bob" or "Bishop John" (see Matt. 23:7–12). A church's pastor (singular) is typically expected to function as a CEO to supervise its staff for the running of its departments and programs. And the members of that church observe, critique, and vote on their performance—with their feet and pocketbooks, if not by formal ballot.

Please don't miss the point here. I accept that the passing of time and the emerging of new cultural patterns can be appealed to for the sake of explaining—perhaps even justifying—some or all of the things that have happened across the centuries. After all, church buildings are "innovations" to the church one reads about in the New Testament. Sending people to school to do advanced biblical studies or to study missiology wasn't an option for that church. And I am no more critical of someone being "*the* pastor" of Crosstown Church than of me being "*the* minister" of the Center City Church. I see no reason to be more critical of "Bishop Smith" than "Brother Shelly" as a clergy title. I am certainly aware that independent Community Churches, Roman Catholic Churches, and Presbyterian Churches all have their chain-of-command structures and share a tendency to make Sunday alone the test of Christian devotion. Attenders are faithful members, while those who show up infrequently are variously thought of as careless, wayward, uncommitted, unfaithful, or damned.

One Church's Move to "Amateurize" Ministry

Speaking of Presbyterians, let me point you to what one has had to say on this very point. Harry Heintz is pastor to the Brunswick Presbyterian Church in Troy, New York. More than a decade ago now, I saw a piece he wrote about that church's attempt to move away from "professionalism" in its life to authentically shared passion for serving Christ. As I was finalizing the materials that would be included in this book, I ran across it again and wondered how the project was going—or whether it was still being pursued. A quick Google search took me to the Brunswick Church website and an electronic version of that article. Interestingly, it is posted under the "About Us" tab; if one clicks "Ministers," the article I first saw in 1999 pops up as the church's current statement about ministry. It explains that the ministers of the Brunswick Church are "all who follow Jesus." The statement proceeds to offer an inspiring account of one of the church's core values. Brunswick seeks to "amateurize" its ministry.

> We've established the amateur model of ministry not so much by programs but by a comprehensive understanding of who we are as the people of God. The first specific emphasis is a "putting off."
>
> We de-emphasize titles and avoid using words that suggest divisions in the church. For instance, we have dropped the words *clergy* and *laity* from our vocabulary. Saying "lay people" is really saying "people people." As an adjective, the word *lay* mainly suggests a second-class ministry.
>
> Clergy words had to go, too—titles like *Reverend* and *Doctor* simply aren't needed. We have no parking places reserved for pastors or staff; rather the pastors park in the spaces farthest away. Officers are encouraged to do the same. We removed the "throne" chairs from the platform. And on church retreats, pastors pay the same fees as everyone else.

> The second emphasis is "putting on"—what we honor in congregational life. In our preaching, for example, we interview people, highlight stories from the marketplace, and make work-related applications. The pastoral prayer each week includes an intercession for a segment of the workforce, often informed by local or global events. The closing of every service features these words: "Together we are the ministers of Jesus and his good news. Each one of us is called, gifted, and commissioned for royal service. Let us enter the new week ready to minister in our homes, our neighborhoods, our schools, and our places of work."
>
> The spadework for every sermon is not done by a pastor alone, but by a small group in which non-staff participants outnumber the staff. The one who will be preaching speaks the least and takes the notes. This happens four to six weeks before the worship service, allowing time to flesh out fresh ideas.
>
> Among the key questions are: What does this passage of Scripture say to the seeker, the growing disciple, and the disillusioned believer? What are the marketplace implications of this truth? Our Sunday morning worship has true amateur input; it's not left to professionals. The results are more honest preaching and more responsive worship.[2]

I applaud such an effort to recapture what the earliest church experienced. The first Christians were Spirit-filled amateurs at their God-given tasks. But they turned the world upside down! The role of "professionals" in the ministry of our churches needs desperately to be moved from priestly performance with audience critique to the role of church leaders as Paul understood it. He saw the work of men such as himself as serving "to equip the saints for the work of ministry for building up the body of Christ" (Eph. 4:12). As Heintz reminds readers in a preamble to the statement already quoted, it was professionals who built the Titanic but amateurs who built the ark.

Leadership: Authoritarian vs. Empowering

Following up briefly on the New Testament notion of how leaders function, it seems clear that leadership is meant ultimately to create *consensus activity* in a local church. That is, Jesus Christ is the single and only head of his body. No single person or small group within the Body of Christ—whether considered globally, denominationally, or congregationally—should presume to think for, interpret for, and give orders about what to be or do in the life of a church. There are no junior heads, princes, or secondary lords. There is Jesus; then there are the rest of us. Those among us who have leadership gifts are to exercise them for the sake of building consensus but never as "lording it over those entrusted to you, but being examples to the flock" (1 Pet. 5:3 NIV).

The church is not called to be a religious corporation with the customary managerial structure of a business; it is called to be a priesthood of all believers that respects the relational nature of the church as family. Yes, families have structure. And there is biblical instruction about how leadership works in a family setting. But neither in the church nor in a family is leadership to be understood as autocratic, authoritarian, or oppressive. Leadership in both settings is to be thought of and applied in terms of humility and nurturing, guidance and empowering. Godly leadership in a church will always be committed to the development and deployment of the natural and Spirit-provided gifts of its members, not the protection of its own turf or authority. The leaders' love for Christ is so genuine and obvious that other believers who see their godliness naturally follow them.

An *elder* (in Greek, *presbyteros*) is simply a mature, godly man whose character exhibited over time makes him a worthy example to other believers. A *shepherd* or *pastor* (*poimen*) is someone who feeds, nurtures, and otherwise tends to the needs of God's flock. An *overseer* (*episkopos*) is one who pays attention to, supervises, and otherwise provides guidance for the activity of the larger group. Not one of these biblical terms is hierarchical or smacks of a pecking order within a power structure. They are functional roles in a church's life that barely resemble what those in our culture think of as an "office" or "position of authority."

Suppose we were to take seriously the notion suggested earlier that the first Christians were "Spirit-filled *amateurs* at their task" of spreading the gospel throughout the Roman Empire. As a priesthood of believers through whom divine service was being offered to God constantly, every Christian had a place in the divine plan. The role of leaders—to use Paul's language already cited—was to equip and encourage Christians to do the work of ministry appropriate to Christ's body on earth. Paul's work as an apostle-leader was not to *do* all the priestly work of the church but to train, guide, and nurture the larger church membership to know how to be Christ's representatives (i.e., living sacrifices) in the world.

The *unity* of the church is in a common confession (i.e., Jesus is Lord), common goal (i.e., to honor God in the obedience of faith), and common message (i.e., the gospel). Our *diversity* is our multifaceted giftedness and resulting dispersion to a variety of places, occupations, and spheres of influence throughout the world. The body is not all a hand or eye or foot, but each part contributes to the health and function of the whole. The farmer and the store clerk belong, as well as the apostle and evangelist.

Gifts such as "apostle, prophet, evangelist, and pastor-teacher" are not better than those of nurse, house painter, attorney, and musician. God needs people to represent Jesus Christ in all the places those people go. He wants to place representatives of the Lord Jesus Christ in every field of honorable employment, in all the professions, in the police and fire departments, in sports and entertainment—wherever, in fact, *you* work and live and interact with other human beings. Every part of the body is valuable. Every part has a function for the benefit of the whole. Every part is needed.

A church functioning under this model seeds Christ-presence throughout its larger environment. It showers a community with examples of nonjudgmental moral purity. It spreads the aroma of generosity and kindness through a selfish and competitive culture. It plants ideas about how to work through family problems or survive grief and loss by faith in a loving God. People see Christ in that church—a community of people "all moving rhythmically and easily with each other, efficient and graceful in response to God's Son, fully mature adults, fully developed within and without, fully alive like Christ" (Eph. 4:23 MSG).

The task of church leaders is to keep this ideal alive in the Christian community. To help believers know the value of their witness. To equip and to oversee the process. In a church that is functioning properly, all its members are active. There is not a single man or woman whose assignment is to be a passive onlooker. There is a graceful and rhythmic responsiveness of the entire body to the will of its one head, Jesus Christ.

It was only in the post-Constantinean church that prophets, pastors, and priests became "officers" in the way we have come to understand that term in the modern church.[3] In the varieties of church polity known to both Catholics and Protestants today, there is institutional authority of the sort one tends to read back into the pages of the New Testament. There simply was no such thing, however, as boards and bylaws of the sort we have created. There were no standing offices that had to be filled for three-year terms in order to exist.

Everything the New Testament envisions as leadership and authority should be translated into our experience in terms of *function* instead of office, *service* rather than status, and *blessing other believers* as opposed to bossing them around. To grasp the difference in the two models, we would be wise to recast our notion of church leadership in terms of *verbs* rather than *nouns*.

All spiritual leadership that honors God is ultimately the influence someone has on others by virtue of his or her faith, character, and devotion to Christ exhibited over time. It can't be conferred in an ordination service; it has to be earned over time. It isn't delegated by vote; it arises from a spiritual life that can no more be hidden from view than a lit candle put on a stand in the middle of the room. It is not designated by a title; it becomes obvious over time through service, faithfulness, and Christlikeness.

Because these things are true of spiritual leadership, it is my conviction that the designation of a church's leaders—as pastors, teachers, deacons, preachers, administrators, and the like—is the natural public recognition of persons who are already performing the tasks of nurturing, communicating the Word of God effectively, ministering to needy or discouraged souls, and so on. Against the view that we see an office or task that needs filling, tap a person on the shoulder, and ordain him or her to that ministry, I suspect the biblical model works in reverse. The person God has gifted and called to a particular leadership function in the church is gradually recognized, affirmed, and publicly commissioned (i.e., appointed, ordained) to it on behalf of the group.

One could object by pointing to New Testament texts that refer to persons who hold a certain "office" in the church. Yet the original text has no word corresponding to "office" and more literally says this: "If someone aspires to overseeing (in Greek, *episkope*), he desires a good work."[4] While office (i.e., status, rank, institutional position) and function (i.e., task, assignment, charge) are certainly not mutually exclusive, the "bishopric" or "monarchical episcopate" as a standing office of institutional power in the church awaited the fourth-century recasting of the church form in order to flourish.

There is no single, fixed pattern of church leadership to be read off the pages of the New Testament. The very notion of finding such a "pattern" is a product of Modernity's penchant for reducing all things—including the spiritual life of the Family of God—to an institutional flowchart. One certainly gets the impression from reading the New Testament that while a church-planting evangelist such as Titus—much less a church-planting apostle such as Paul—provided strong personal leadership in establishing a new church, one of his first and most important duties was to pass the leadership mantle to a group of men[5] whose devotion to Christ had set them apart for oversight and nurturing within the church. "The reason I left you in Crete," Paul told Titus by letter, "was that you might straighten out what was left unfinished and appoint elders in every town, as I directed you" (Tit. 1:5 NIV; see Acts 14:21–23).

The leadership paradigm for the Church of Sanctified Religiosity is clearly *authoritarian* in nature. There is a tiny base of leaders at the top of a hierarchical pyramid. Decisions are made by a single strong individual or by a group of lordly officials and communicated by fiat. The leadership body then presses others who have attached to the group either to conform or to get out. Alternate ideas are discouraged. Limited options are open to members. As a result of this authoritarian model of leadership, dysfunctional persons tend to rise to power. And the goal of such dysfunctional persons is to create a solid following within the "system" in order to hold and extend power. Experiences with leadership that functions on this authoritarian model are common in government and education, business and the professions. They are also common and well-known in religion.

But a different paradigm for *empowering* leadership is presenting itself in the healthier relational context that is emerging. A collegial respect for members is fostered at all levels of age and education, wealth and talent. Persons emerge as leaders within the group on the basis of their character over time and for their demonstrated ability to build consensus within the group. Diversity is not only tolerated by such leaders but valued and respected. Alternate ideas are welcomed. Members of the larger group are given a variety of options—because the leaders are not trying to advance their personal agenda or prestige but to enlarge ministry participation by the community as a whole. Dysfunctional people stand out negatively in such a community and are held accountable to it. Leaders who emerge in these churches see their goal as nurturing the gifts of others in a relational context. Thus they facilitate and oversee churches who live the practical meaning of the priesthood of all believers.

Authoritarian leadership by a command-and-control model will destroy a family, business, or church—even if it seems to thrive for a period of time. An environment in which the many serve the will of the few is unhealthy. It contains within itself the seeds of its own destruction. Empowering leadership honors God by respecting his people, sanctioning the gifts he has distributed among them, and using godly good judgment to oversee their coordination with one another.

This chapter began by claiming that Jesus' idea of leadership was at odds with those most current at his time. Keep that in mind as you read these words from Jesus:

> You've observed how godless rulers throw their weight around, how quickly a little power goes to their heads. It's not going to be that way with you. Whoever wants to be great must become a servant. Whoever wants to be first among you must be your slave. That is what the Son of Man has done: He came to serve, not be served—and then to give away his life in exchange for the many who are held hostage. (Matt. 20:25b–28 MSG)

The model for Christian leadership here seems clear. It is not authoritarian and abusive. To the contrary, it is empowering. It is leadership that gives itself away for the sake of others rather than leadership that pushes others around.

Community of the Dispersed

As post-Reformation churches have generally interpreted the doctrine of the priesthood of all believers, we have missed half—if not fully two-thirds—of the biblical idea. The part we have gotten right is that every Christian has direct and unmediated access to God through Christ. We do not need human priests to mediate for us. We certainly do not need the once-for-all sacrifice of Jesus for sin offered again and again on our behalf (see Heb. 10:12–18).

The part we seem not to have grasped and implemented is that the priestly ministry of every Christian is to perform a God-honoring, Christ-exalting function in the world. As our one and all-sufficient high priest, Jesus made an offering of his own body to God on our behalf. From his exalted place at the right hand of the Father, he is still our high priest who is offering his body (i.e., the church) for the sake of the world. In practical terms, this means that every believer is expected to offer her or his body as a living sacrifice to God (see Rom. 12:1).

It is a mistake of monumental proportions to think that the priestly ministry of the church is a Sunday-focused event. It is the whole life of the whole church that is our living-body sacrifice to the Lord. Sunday praise is to be joined with Tuesday work and Thursday golf, Wednesday family life and Saturday yard work. Everything in the life of a Christian is to be seamless in terms of its appropriateness for displaying the excellence of God's heart and character. Yes, the church is sometimes a *gathered* community for the purpose of assembly, praise, and ministry. More often, however, it is what the Reformer Melancthon called "the community of the dispersed." The arena within which the church functions to put the holiness of God on display is the world—to which it is light and for whose sake it is salt and leaven. If we think of ourselves as church only when we are within four walls, who is doing God's work "out there"?

Luis Palau makes this point with a metaphor most of us would understand. He says the church is like manure. Spread it around, and it will give life, make things grow, and produce fruit. Keep it all collected in one place, and it stinks! Yes, we need preachers and musicians, pastors and deacons. But what we really need is for all of us to be worthy representatives of our Lord Christ at our desks and on the phone, making a frustrated customer feel valued for her business or a frightened patient feel cared for as a person. We need every Christian treating strangers as if we knew we were welcoming angels onto earth. We need the mindset that produces teachers and bank presidents, janitors and celebrities, teenagers and senior citizens whose conscious goal in life is to be a living sacrifice to God.

A third truth I suspect we have missed because of Modernity's peculiar take on the gospel is that our priesthood is communal in nature, not individualistic. My fear is that most of our appeal to this doctrine has been for the sake of "private interpretation of Scripture" and a resulting fragmentation of the Body of Christ. What the Reformers called "the priesthood of all believers" (i.e., communal function) was bastardized by the Enlightenment to become "the priesthood of the believer" (i.e., rugged individualism) and progressively degenerated into a belief in the right of every tub to sit on its own bottom. What a scandalous outcome to so holy a beginning. A positive contribution of postmodernity could be to point us back to the importance of community in our faith.

On Peter's view of the matter, the obvious priority for all who love Christ is "sincere love" (1 Pet. 1:22b NIV) for their brothers and sisters in Christ's spiritual body. The first and second commandments about loving God completely and loving neighbors as ourselves have come together in the church. Believers in community are learning to "love one another deeply, from the heart" (1:22c). What a contrast that community is to the one around it. Hearts that have been purified by their obedience to the truth are modeling an alternative reality to a world too familiar with envy and competition. They rejoice with those who rejoice and weep with those who weep—rather than weep with frustration over another's success or laugh with glee over that same person's pain. They bear one another's burdens. They expend the energy of their lives on behalf of one another. The world watches and says, "Look how those Christians love one another!" That is, in fact, the very thing Tertullian (ca. 200) said unbelievers said of the church of his own time.

For centuries under the Law of Moses, worshippers had thought to please God with sacrifices and burnt offerings. It didn't work! Lives had not been transformed. Redemptive community had not been created. Outsiders had mocked and even tormented rather than desired to be part of Israel. And Israel had reacted by isolating and insulating itself from the Gentile nations. All this had defeated God's purpose for the Jews. He had wanted to make them a light to the nations. He made them his Chosen People that they might become the beating heart of an entire world living to the glory of God.

The key truth the Israelites of old had missed was that Yahweh had always wanted their hearts and not their cattle, their bodies and not their burnt offerings. At least, that is what the Book of Hebrews says (see Heb. 10:5–10). According to that preacher, Christ's unique understanding of the Father is what allowed him to offer the perfect sacrifice. And that sacrifice was doing the will of God—not sacrifices and offerings. Surrender to God as the one sure reality. Obeying the truth. Since he was called to be our Great High Priest by virtue of this insight, we are not surprised that those who believe in him are called to offer the same sacrifice—their "bodies as a living sacrifice" (Rom. 12:1).

Peter shares this understanding of priesthood and sacrifice. So he calls the dispersed believers to whom he writes his letter to one-another love, one-another purity, and one-another nurture. The result would be church as a priesthood of all believers—"a holy priesthood, offering spiritual sacrifices acceptable to God through Jesus Christ" (1 Pet. 2:5b NIV). Functioning in this way, the church would not only be an alternative community that models kingdom life but also an evangelistic witness—"a royal priesthood" whose activity will "proclaim the mighty acts of him who called you out of darkness into his marvelous light" (2:9). Acutely aware of our status as "aliens and strangers in the world"—because our citizenship is in heaven—our daily life-sacrifice shows what it is to be priests of God. Negatively, we draw on the power of the Spirit to abstain from God-denying desires so common and constant in this hostile environment (2:11); positively, we maintain a lifestyle that reflects our heavenly citizenship and which causes people to give honor to God (2:12).

In Revelation, the final book of the New Testament, this motif of church as a priesthood of all believers is also stressed. When Jesus first appears in the apocalyptic drama as the Risen and Triumphant Lamb of God, a "new song" is sung to honor him for his redemptive work among humanity.

> You are worthy to take the scroll
> and to open its seals,
> because you were slain,
> and with your blood you purchased men for God
> from every tribe and language and people and nation.
> You have made them to be *a kingdom and priests to serve our God*,
> and they will reign on the earth. (Rev. 5:9–10 NIV, italics added)

As the book moves toward its dramatic conclusion and envisions those who overcome the dragon, beast, and false prophet to stand in triumph with the Lamb, the motif reappears. "Blessed and holy are those who have part in the first resurrection. The second death has no power over them, but *they will be priests of God and of Christ and will reign with him* for a thousand years" (Rev. 20:6 NIV, italics added).

But there is still another side to what Heintz has termed "amateurish ministry." The biblical mandate seems clear now. But think of the practical value of it. A revolutionary enlargement of the church's effectiveness would follow from a genuine priestly service of all believers to the Lord. Not because we "have church" seven days a week but because we understand church isn't just one day a week. Not because we have more paid church staff but because we discover the real job of a church's paid staff is to equip the total membership for ministry. And not because we send more church members to retreats and conferences but because we send them to their normal, everyday places with a sense of real mission.

Going back to Martin Luther, his point about the priesthood of all believers seems not only to have been that a farmer who plows his field or a girl who milks cows should be permitted to do things that were permitted only to ordained priests in his day (which Luther surely believed) but also that the farmer plowing or the girl working as a milkmaid is doing priestly work in those pursuits. God help us all to grasp this important point!

In the first place, what holier work is there on Earth than that of a mother nursing her baby or changing his diaper or keeping the home environment cheerful for all its members? Isn't a nurse or physician doing God's healing work in the world? So why isn't a policeman or fireman doing God's protective work? A janitor his environmental work? A grocer his food distribution? A mechanic his helping and repair work? The point is every facet of a Christian's life has a worshipful dimension. It is part of her priestly offering to God. It is what he does to help people see Christ's presence in the world.

If that sounds too idealistic, it is only because we have lost sight of an important truth about the church as God's priesthood. God values every one of us in whatever it is we do in our occupations and daily routines. Our High Priest has raised the ordinary things of our lives to the level of a priestly offering, a divine vocation. God can be glorified in everything you do that is honorable on Planet Earth. Or, to say the same thing in reverse, anything that cannot be offered to him as priestly service is thereby judged inappropriate and dishonorable for us.

Paul once wrote to a young, immature church where some members who had experienced divine gifting for speaking in tongues or teaching the Word of God had morphed into super-Christians. They were contemptuous of people who didn't have their abilities. They were neglecting their families in favor of their gifts. They were getting contemptuous of their daily routines of ordinary work. (Sounds like they had aspirations to become "clergy," doesn't it?) Here was Paul's counsel: "So, dear brothers and sisters, whatever situation you were in when you became a believer, stay there in your new relationship with God" (1 Cor. 7:24 NLT).

Paul didn't write that to keep the number of Christian ministers to a minimum. To the contrary, he said it to help Christians realize that they are all ministers. All servants. All priests. He wasn't "putting them down," but raising them up—helping them see that God values and works through all of us! There is no clergy-laity distinction in his scheme of things. This is the same apostle's authoritative word in another of his letters: "Whatever you do, work at it with all your heart, as working for the Lord, not for men, since you know that you will receive an inheritance from the Lord as a reward. It is the Lord Christ you are serving" (Col. 3:23–24 NIV). Can you take that to work with you tomorrow morning? Can you believe that what you will be doing Sunday morning is as important in God's scheme of redemption as what you are doing Thursday morning? It is. It *really* is.

It is humanly impossible for the "ordained clergy" of a city to be in all the places where God will need someone to function as a representative of his Beloved Son. He will need someone in the flower shop, at the service station, in your office, on your bus, in a hospital waiting room—all over the city. Your routine may carry you to one of those places. And your high calling as a priest of God is to offer service there. You may not say a prayer. You may not read a Bible verse. You might not mention the name of Jesus. You probably won't get a handshake at the door or a pat on the back for what you do. But in abstaining from evil desires, doing your task with integrity, and otherwise being Christ's representative in those places, you will have fulfilled your calling as a priest on duty for the Lord.

My role as a preacher on a given Sunday morning is not to offer my audience a religious devotional speech to critique but to make good spiritual use of my gift with words. I remind others to make equally good spiritual use of their gifts for banking, parenting, teaching, repairing cars, building houses, selling real estate, or whatever else God has gifted them to do. In fact, I keep this note inside a folder in which I sometimes carry my sermon notes. I use it to remind me to remind others to be God's person outside the church walls.

As we enter the world today, let us pray for God to:

Send us to his places
to do his things
in his ways
for his purposes and
to his glory!

May it be so for you in your place today and for me in mine. Both settings are holy to the Lord.

Chapter Twelve

Turning Church Upside Down

"So many of the selfless people
serving the world's neediest are
lowly nuns and priests—notable
not for the grandeur of their vestments
but for the grandness of their compassion."
—Nicholas Kristof

When you hear the word *church*, what comes to mind? What do you visualize? What images dominate?

Some people will visualize a structure. For them, church is a building with high ceilings, stained glass windows, and a steeple. It is where people gather on Sunday morning to sing or listen to religious instruction. They may or may not be involved with anything that happens there. Perhaps they give directions in relation to it. "Go north from here for three or four blocks. Watch for a white church on the left side of the street, and turn right immediately past it."

For these people, church is a building on a piece of property that is dedicated to religious events. So "church planting" is when a group of people—perhaps dissatisfied with the religious events that take place on the property to which they have been driving on Sundays—gets together, identifies a piece of property, buys it, erects a building (with predictable architectural features), and puts up a sign announcing times of services to be conducted there.

That leads, in turn, to a second notion of church as religious services, meetings, and assembly times. So we have such common expressions as "getting to church on time" or "going to church." We may have a specific place in mind, but the idea in these expressions is an event that starts at a certain time—and ends before the Methodists (or Catholics or Baptists) fill up all the good restaurants. And it wouldn't count as "church" unless the event had certain features such as Bible reading, music with biblical-religious themes, and prayer. Without those characteristic features packaged in a reasonably familiar way, people leave the event and say things like, "I don't even feel like I've been to church today!"

There is also the notion of church as a broad social movement or political activity. Historians may speak of things like the impact of the church on life in the Middle Ages or the decline of the church's influence in France. A newspaper story may say that divorce rates are no lower among people who are church members in America than in the general population—and slightly higher in some regions of the country.

It is true that the church can use a building and property for holy purposes; but the building and property are not really the church. Right? The church is the group of people who sometimes makes use of land and buildings but is not identical to them. It is true that churches have meetings and do things with a particularly religious flavor during those meeting times; but it would be a mistake to think that the church doesn't exist when it is not gathered in one location. And it is also correct that one can look at social influences tied to the activity of people who are acting in the name of Christ or under the authority of a church; there have been positive influences such as hospitals and charitable works that would not have been created without church initiative, and there have been such terribly negative things as crusades and murders.

A Different Way to Think of Church

But what if the church were not a building or meeting time. Not a "power bloc" vying for influence and votes within the world's political structures? Not a self-serving institution whose central goal is maintenance of property, status, and budgets? What if the church were a microcosm of the kingdom of God that focuses the great variety of personalities, gifts, and passions of people to the single task of honoring God in the world? With different groups of Christians seeing the good in one another? With all of them looking for ways to serve and honor the non-Christians around them? What if the church were to embrace a lifestyle of humility and obedience, faith and love, integrity and virtue—concerned more to be the Living Body of Christ than to own property or hold big rallies or sway the outcome of political contests?

The church is supposed to be a pilgrim-community of people so deeply committed to Christ that we are collectively a "third race of humanity"—beyond the customary biblical categories of Jew and Gentile—in which God can put on display the life he originally intended everyone to experience. And that life is not that of an isolated individual standing against the world so much as it is the closeness of people to God and one another that lets them experience fulfillment, joy, and divine presence in the world. Yes, the pilgrimage eventually leads to heaven. But the journey itself is hardly inconsequential to the outcome. The total process is participation with God in his purpose to make all things whole and holy. To bring *shalom* into human lives. To create relationships that are wholesome and loving and in which people try to outdo each other in showing kindness and respect.

Biblical theology begins in the paradise of the Garden of Eden. God and the creatures he had made in his very own image and likeness were going to live in open dialogue, productivity, and joy. The Earth would be God's, no less than Heaven. His bidding would be done by angels and humans. Male and female. Young and old. But the process was spoiled when Adam and Eve misused their freedom and introduced sin, flight from God, and self-will into the equation. Since that faulty beginning, God has been working to restore things to their original purpose.

So the Old Testament prophets grimly reflect the murder, sensuality, and godlessness of their times. But they keep pointing with hope to a situation that will be known as the Kingdom of God—the Reign of God, the Supremacy of God, the Blessed Nearness of God—among humankind. Isaiah explains how Yahweh chose a small and minor ethnic group to whom he would reveal himself and through whom he would model this kingdom to other nations—who then would want to be part of the same experience. Israel would be a "light for the Gentiles" for bringing Yahweh's "salvation to the ends of the earth" (see Isa. 49:6).

Jesus likened this project to God having planted a beautiful vineyard and giving it to Israel to tend. The outcome would be a beautiful attraction whose fruit could be enjoyed by every nation, tongue, and tribe. Even so, that project came to a sad and unhappy end.

> Jesus said, "Listen to another parable: There was a landowner who planted a vineyard. He put a wall around it, dug a winepress in it and built a watchtower. Then he rented the vineyard to some farmers and went away on a journey. When the harvest time approached, he sent his servants to the tenants to collect his fruit.
>
> "The tenants seized his servants; they beat one, killed another, and stoned a third. Then he sent other servants to them, more than the first time, and the tenants treated them the same way. Last of all, he sent his son to them. 'They will respect my son,' he said.
>
> "But when the tenants saw the son, they said to each other, 'This is the heir. Come, let's kill him and take his inheritance.' So they took him and threw him out of the vineyard and killed him.

"Therefore, when the owner of the vineyard comes, what will he do to those tenants?"

"He will bring those wretches to a wretched end," they replied, "and he will rent the vineyard to other tenants, who will give him his share of the crop at harvest time."

Jesus said to them, "Have you never read in the Scriptures:

"'The stone the builders rejected
has become the capstone;
the Lord has done this,
and it is marvelous in our eyes'?" (Matt. 21:33–42 NIV)

This parable traces the history of God's redemptive work, as he sent first one and then another prophet to Israel over time. Those prophets were rejected in a variety of impious ways. Finally, God came in person. Jesus of Nazareth was Immanuel (i.e., God with us) to show what the kingdom of God would look like in human form. So he wasn't rich or powerful, pushy or menacing. He was, however, magnetic in his presence by virtue of purity, kindness, and generosity. His announced goal was to begin calling people from all sorts of backgrounds into a single, multiethnic community that would follow him, reproduce what he had started on Planet Earth, and give anyone drawn to that community the right to participate in the same experience. That experience is what the Scripture calls the kingdom of God or the kingdom of heaven.

So Isaiah looked beyond the shortcomings and rebellions of his own time and anticipated what would happen when Jesus Messiah appeared. In one place, he gives this generic announcement of heaven's intention to do something radical. Something both startling and refreshing. Something so wondrous that the whole creation would be returned to its purpose of giving glory to God at every level—human beings, animal life, trees and rivers, the very planet itself.

> See, I am doing a new thing!
> Now it springs up; do you not perceive it?
> I am making a way in the desert
> and streams in the wasteland.
> The wild animals honor me,
> the jackals and the owls,
> because I provide water in the desert
> and streams in the wasteland,
> to give drink to my people, my chosen,
> the people I formed for myself
> that they may proclaim my praise. (Isa. 43:19–21 NIV)

In an even more graphic and detailed picture of what life would be like in the Age of Messiah, the same prophet wrote:

> "Behold, I will create
> new heavens and a new earth.
> The former things will not be remembered,
> nor will they come to mind.
> But be glad and rejoice forever
> in what I will create,
> for I will create Jerusalem to be a delight
> and its people a joy.
> I will rejoice over Jerusalem
> and take delight in my people;
> the sound of weeping and of crying
> will be heard in it no more.
>
> "Never again will there be in it
> an infant who lives but a few days,
> or an old man who does not live out his years;
> he who dies at a hundred

> will be thought a mere youth;
> he who fails to reach a hundred
> will be considered accursed.
> They will build houses and dwell in them;
> they will plant vineyards and eat their fruit.
> No longer will they build houses and others live in them,
> or plant and others eat.
> For as the days of a tree,
> so will be the days of my people;
> my chosen ones will long enjoy
> the works of their hands.
> They will not toil in vain
> or bear children doomed to misfortune;
> for they will be a people blessed by the Lord,
> they and their descendants with them.
> Before they call I will answer;
> while they are still speaking I will hear.
> The wolf and the lamb will feed together,
> and the lion will eat straw like the ox,
> but dust will be the serpent's food.
> They will neither harm nor destroy
> on all my holy mountain,"
> says the Lord. (Isa. 65:17–25 NIV)

Jesus summarized the situation he had come to address with this metaphor:

> Jesus told them another parable: "The kingdom of heaven is like a man who sowed good seed in his field. But while everyone was sleeping, his enemy came and sowed weeds among the wheat, and went away. When the wheat sprouted and formed heads, then the weeds also appeared.

> "The owner's servants came to him and said, 'Sir, didn't you sow good seed in your field? Where then did the weeds come from?'
>
> "'An enemy did this,' he replied.
>
> "The servants asked him, 'Do you want us to go and pull them up?'
>
> "'No,' he answered, 'because while you are pulling the weeds, you may root up the wheat with them. Let both grow together until the harvest. At that time I will tell the harvesters: First collect the weeds and tie them in bundles to be burned; then gather the wheat and bring it into my barn.'" (Matt. 13:24–30 NIV)

But you and I are trying to figure out where we are in this scenario. We are trying to understand where the church fits within this larger picture of God's purpose in history. And what is the church's relationship to the kingdom of God?

The Church Is Central to God's Plan

Because sin is not part of the reign of God and because, in fact, the wages of sin is death, Jesus offered his life redemptively at the cross. All the animal sacrifices that had been required from antiquity through the time of Abraham and under the Law of Moses had been designed to communicate this message: *sin breaks one's relationship with God, and healing so great a breach is incredibly costly*. Money won't do it. Good deeds aren't sufficient. Even tears cried sincerely cannot undo the harm that has been done. In a word: "The soul who sins is the one who will die" (Ezek. 18:20a NIV)—not the child for the parent, not the lover for the beloved. The guilt of sin is personal. So each person must be held accountable for his or her offense against the rule of God in his or her life.

Yet the theme of Scripture is the redemption of sinful humanity by the grace of God. God is not one of the pagan deities—which were never anything other than the fantasy creations of humans who corrupted the intuitive awareness of God everyone possesses (see Rom. 1:20–21). The worst features of those pagan gods were, in fact, their petulance and rage, their bloodlust and malevolence. The One True God who reveals himself as *holy* in his hatred for sin—on account of what it does not to him but to the humans he loves—also shows himself *loving* and *gracious* by providing the means by which a sinner who justly deserves to die is mercifully allowed to live. "For the life of a creature is in the blood, and I have given it to you to make atonement for yourselves on the altar; it is the blood that makes atonement for one's life" (Lev. 17:11 NIV).

Follow the narrative in its development:

- God created us in his image to live in perfect harmony with him and one another.
- The essence of human sin—whether Adam's or mine or yours—is a rejection of God's kingly rule.
- Although divine holiness will not allow God to ignore our sin, his grace makes him determined to redeem us from it.
- The legitimate penalty for sin is death, so God mercifully allowed human beings to substitute the life of an animal that could be sacrificed in place of the sinful person's own soul.
- God himself creates and supplies the animals to us and allows their blood to be shed at an altar—from which a human worshipper comes away with sins atoned for (i.e., covered) by grace.
- Since sacrificing animals for humans was not sufficient, God ultimately took human form to offer his own body as a once-for-all atonement (Heb. 10:1-10).

Every person who accepts this redemptive narrative by faith as his or her own is justified on the basis of Christ's redeeming work. His personal holiness is credited to every person who is willing to repent of the sin that required such a sacrifice of him. That is why one of the fundamental messages of redemption takes this form: "The kingdom of God is near. Repent and believe the good news!" (Mark 1:15 NIV).

Every person saved by this "good news" (i.e., gospel) is simultaneously added to the church, the Body of Christ. The now-living, now-reigning Anointed One of God imparts his resurrection life to those people. He not only forgives our past, but he also begins the process of renewing us so we can bear the image and likeness of God for which we were created. We are given—remember the language now of Isaiah about the "new thing" (43:19) Yahweh was going to do and the joyous life he would give his people in the new-Jerusalem community (65:18)—newness of life in Christ. So Paul writes: "Therefore, if anyone is in Christ, he is a new creation; the old has gone, the new has come! All this is from God, who reconciled us to himself through Christ and gave us the ministry of reconciliation: that God was reconciling the world to himself in Christ, not counting men's sins against them" (2 Cor. 5:17–19 NIV).

Redemption and Reconciliation

The term "reconciliation" is important to New Testament theology. Counter to the spirit of some ideas of holiness as personal isolation or monastic retreat into the desert, the biblical idea of salvation involves a renewal of healthy community. Men and women are not only reconciled to God through the work of Jesus Christ but to one another as well. Rodney Clapp states the biblical perspective this way:

> The Bible knows nothing of preoccupation with the isolated, acultural individual and his or her inwardness. It instead shows a keen and abiding concern with time and place, with unfolding history, human societies and physical creation. The goal or proper end of human life, according to the Old Testament, is not the individual soul's flight from the constraints of time

> and body. It is instead the enjoyment of wholeness in communion with God and God's people, amid a healed and no longer strife-driven creation. In this enduring Jewish tradition, the New Testament looks ahead to the communal resurrection of those redeemed in Christ (1 Cor 15) and longs for the healing of the "whole creation" (Rom 8:18–30).[1]

Because this is so, the church stands as a witness to the larger culture about what is possible for those who have not yet repented of their self-directed lives in order to believe the good news that God's kingdom rule is yet possible. All those "in Christ" are commissioned to model and to declare, to experience and to offer the newness of life that is the kingdom of God. No single event can summarize this commission; it is a lifelong process that includes spiritual formation in all the ways Jesus showed his original disciples. That is why another way of summarizing the preaching of the gospel takes this form: "Go out and train everyone you meet, far and near, in this way of life, marking them by baptism in the threefold name: Father, Son, and Holy Spirit. Then instruct them in the practice of all I have commanded you. I'll be with you as you do this, day after day after day, right up to the end of the age" (Matt. 28:19–20 MSG).

The church is *not* buildings and property. It is *not* religious assemblies and ceremonies. It is *not* alignment with certain social causes or political parties. The church is a community of redeemed people in process of daily surrender to God's rule. The church is—in the version of Matthew just quoted—a distinctive "way of life" being modeled by the already-Christians to the not-yet-Christians. To quote Clapp again, "The church must indeed be the message it wishes a watchful world to hear and embrace."[2] The church is Christ's "second incarnation" in the world. It offers a practicable vision of the kingdom of God in microcosm as an invitation for others to come and share.

Yes, the full and complete redemption of this fallen world must await the return of Christ. The final enemy (i.e., death) will not be destroyed until his coming. But the church is called to put on display the sort of purity, joy, generosity, and holiness that reveals God to those who either do not know him or whose vision of him has been distorted by pagan (i.e., angry, vindictive) or sub-Christian (i.e., self-serving, self-righteous) distortions of his nature and will.

Think of the world into which Christianity was born. It was remarkable for its divisions. The division between rich and poor was huge—with perhaps more than half of the population of the Roman Empire being slaves at the time. The rich lived in extreme indulgence and open debauchery. Abortion and infanticide were widespread, and infants—girls in particular—were abandoned to slavery or prostitution. Women were exploited. Entertainment was violent, sensual, bloody, and vulgar. Political intrigue was rife—leading not only to the crucifixion of Jesus under Pontius Pilate but the persecution and martyrdom of many Christians in generations to follow.

The church was offered to that world as an alternative community, an alternative way of life. They specifically countered all the divisions in first-century society with community "in Christ." "You are all sons of God through faith in Christ Jesus, for all of you who were baptized into Christ have clothed yourselves with Christ. There is neither Jew nor Greek, slave nor free, male nor female, for you are all one in Christ Jesus" (Gal. 3:27–28 NIV).

In the midst of all this, the church developed a self-image.

> But even if you suffer for doing what is right, God will reward you for it. So don't be afraid and don't worry. Instead, you must worship Christ as Lord of your life. And if you are asked about your Christian hope, always be ready to explain it. But you must do this in a gentle and respectful way. Keep your conscience clear.

> Then if people speak evil against you, they will be ashamed when they see what a good life you live because you belong to Christ. Remember, it is better to suffer for doing good, if that is what God wants, than to suffer for doing wrong! (1 Pet. 3:14–17 NLT)

The Christians used a term of themselves that was already in the vocabulary of the time. "Resident aliens" were people living in a given country who had none of the rights of citizenship—property ownership, inheritance, defense at trial. So the Christians were taught to think of themselves as citizens of heaven (see Phil. 3:20) who are aliens and strangers in this world.

> I, Peter, am an apostle on assignment by Jesus, the Messiah, writing to exiles scattered to the four winds. Not one is missing, not one forgotten. God the Father has his eye on each of you, and has determined by the work of the Spirit to keep you obedient through the sacrifice of Jesus. May everything good from God be yours! (1 Pet. 1:1–2 MSG)
>
> But you are a chosen people, a royal priesthood, a holy nation, a people belonging to God, that you may declare the praises of him who called you out of darkness into his wonderful light. Once you were not a people, but now you are the people of God; once you had not received mercy, but now you have received mercy.
>
> Dear friends, I urge you, as aliens and strangers in the world, to abstain from sinful desires, which war against your soul. Live such good lives among the pagans that, though they accuse you of doing wrong, they may see your good deeds and glorify God on the day he visits us. (1 Pet. 2:9–12 NIV)
>
> Dear friends, do not be surprised at the painful trial you are suffering, as though something strange were happening to you. But rejoice that you participate in the sufferings of Christ, so that

> you may be overjoyed when his glory is revealed. If you are insulted because of the name of Christ, you are blessed, for the Spirit of glory and of God rests on you. If you suffer, it should not be as a murderer or thief or any other kind of criminal, or even as a meddler. However, if you suffer as a Christian, do not be ashamed, but praise God that you bear that name. (1 Pet. 4:12–16 NIV)

What God does to restore humanity on a personal, individual level is a microcosm of what he proposes to do for the Body of Christ at large. What he does for the Body of Christ at a corporate level is what he will eventually do for all of creation. In the meanwhile, the individual believer, the waiting church, and all creation is "groaning as in the pains of childbirth" (Rom. 8:22 NIV).

The Loss of Countercultural Presence

With the imprint left by Constantine, however, this vision for the church faded. The church lost its identity as an organism and became an organization. It lost its virtue as the corporate expression of Christ and turned into a religious corporation. The church abandoned its calling to be a microcosm of the kingdom reign of God for the sake of becoming a location, an event to witness, a political force, or an entity whose favor could be courted by the world. Church gradually ceased being countercultural and became the dominant culture.

Over time, a theology emerged that absolutized church over kingdom. That distorted theology prioritized church membership over Spirit-transformed personality. It recast leadership from Spirit-empowered function to titles and offices. It eventually changed corporate worship from participation to passivity and reduced the larger concept of worship from whole-life sacrifice to God to a time-bounded event.

What emerged was an institution whose members were taught to divide life into sacred and secular, ordained and non-clerical, clergy and laity. So what happens between 9 a.m. and noon on Sundays is spiritual and belongs to God; what takes place in the lives of Sunday morning worshippers during the balance of the week is not critical to faith and status in the church. The money you deposit in a collection plate on Sunday is God's; the remainder of your income and the things you do with it are yours.

Along the way in Christian history, the church morphed into something more like a business or government than the living, breathing Body of Christ in the world. Christians became consumers, and churches competed with one another to sell their theology, their worship, and their ability to meet felt needs. God never willed for such things to happen. He meant for the church to be a microcosm of the kingdom of God and to put the holiness, generosity, and service to others Jesus modeled on display to all centuries and peoples.

There are people today who are hearing the call of Jesus to whole-life discipleship and a new vision of church. And they are turning the church upside down. All Christians are included in the vision of a relational church these people have received from God; church membership as to denomination, nondenomination, or congregation is marginal to kingdom obedience. Greatness in this church is not about rank or title but submission to God and service to people. Spirituality is not an inner aspect of a Christian's life but is our everyday lifestyle, God-honoring vocabulary, and Christ-like acceptance of people others either fail to notice or refuse to acknowledge. It is not the invisible part of us that we nurture in rarified, relaxed moments but the relationship of our embodied selves to God and others that is eternal life here and now in the material world. Salvation is not what we get when this life is over but what we experience as our lives are delivered from the empty, unholy way of thinking and behaving and treating one another that dominates human history and culture.

Nicholas Kristof is not a Christian apologist, and the *New York Times* is not a theological journal. While writing about an impoverished and ravaged southern Sudan, however, Kristof made the point of this book to the readers of that newspaper. Writing specifically of some works he encountered in Sudan that were being done by Catholic workers, he noted "there seem to be two Catholic Churches, the old boys' club of the Vatican and the grass-roots network of humble priests, nuns and laity in places like Sudan." While expressing his view that the Roman Catholic Church has a hierarchy "whose apex is male chauvinist, homophobic and so out of touch," he nevertheless applauds those humble priests, nuns, and laity of Catholicism who turn their backs on church politics for the sake of compassion that models the heart of Christ to the world.

> Jesus wasn't known for pontificating from palaces, covering up scandals, or issuing Paleolithic edicts on social issues. Does anyone think he would have protected clergymen who raped children?
>
> Yet if the top of the church has strayed from its roots, much of its base is still deeply inspiring. I came here to impoverished southern Sudan to write about Sudanese problems, not the Catholic Church's. Yet once again, I am awed that so many of the selfless people serving the world's neediest are lowly nuns and priests—notable not for the grandeur of their vestments but for the grandness of their compassion.[3]

Kristof quotes one nun who told him "she worries sometimes that if Jesus returned he would say, 'Oh, they got it all wrong!'" Indeed, to the degree that our concern—whether Catholic, Protestant, or nondenominational—has ever been status, vestments, titles, size of congregation, or amount of collections, Christianity in whatever form has indeed got it all wrong. On the other hand, Spirit-filled, self-emptying, other-devoted, and God-honoring souls who care for none of those things know Jesus and are putting his kingdom on display for the world.

Capturing the Ancient Vision

Sometime in the second century, an apologist for the Christian faith wrote to a government official to argue against the view that the church was somehow a threat to the state. His words seem appropriate to quote here to give a glimpse of how some early believers saw the role of the church as a microcosm of the kingdom of God.

> Christians cannot be distinguished from the rest of the human race by country or language or customs. They do not live in cities of their own; they do not use a peculiar form of speech; they do not follow an eccentric manner of life. . . .
>
> Every foreign land is their fatherland, and yet for them every fatherland is a foreign land. They marry, like everyone else, and they beget children, but they do not cast out their offspring. They share their board with each other, but not their marriage bed. It is true that they are "in the flesh," but they do not live "according to the flesh." They busy themselves on earth, but their citizenship is in heaven. They obey the established laws, but in their own lives they go far beyond what the laws require. . . .
>
> To put it simply: What the soul is in the body, that Christians are in the world. The soul is dispersed through all the members of the body, and Christians are scattered through all the cities of the world. The soul dwells in the body, but does not belong to the body, and the Christians dwell in the world, but do not belong to the world.[4]

Christians belong in the marketplace of ideas to be what Martin Luther dubbed "a sort of Christ" there. But we have turned churches into Christian ghettos and isolated ourselves from the world. We have put our hope in Sunday morning worship in church-owned properties rather than in the power of the Holy Spirit to disperse us into all the places we go to demonstrate that the One in us is greater than the Evil One who is prince of this world. We have lost our vision of Jesus for the sake of advancing Christianity.

We need to implement an authentic priesthood of all believers. Go into our offices, homes, classrooms, and workplaces as Christ's servants. Go there in the humility of the Son of Man. Offer no judgments or directives; be confessional about our own inadequacies and modest about our accomplishments. We should not ask to speak; we should be Christ's presence so authentically that we will be asked to explain ourselves. Then we bear gentle, faithful witness to the one who is our Lord.

Such persons would be called anything but self-righteous hypocrites. In their reverent use of the name of Jesus, they would receive a more respectful hearing than is the case in so many venues where the Church of Sanctified Religiosity intrudes today.

If the claim that the earliest church was "turning the world upside down" was true in its time (see Acts 17:6), it certainly is *not* true today. The church is often viewed as nothing more than an irrelevance by our world. So perhaps it is the church that needs to be turned upside down—divesting itself of the pagan style of leadership that puts the powerful few at the top and embracing the Jesus style of leadership that understands serving as leading and humility as greatness.

May it be so in our own time—and until he comes. Only then may we be said to be praying with authenticity the words of the Lord's Prayer: "Your kingdom come, your will be done on earth as it is in heaven."

Conclusion

"Our fulfillment is in offering emptiness,
our usefulness in becoming useless,
our power in becoming powerless."
—Henri J. M. Nouwen

A word used so frequently of Christ's disciples in the New Testament that we tend to overlook its significance is *diakonoi*. Apostles, leaders in local churches, prophets, tongues-speakers, persons gifted to heal the sick, people who make clothing or food for the poor, teachers, ordinary folk who loved Jesus—all were regarded as *ministers* or *servants* to the Son of God. At the opening of the chapter in which Paul gives the longer list from which I excerpted only a few examples of *ministry* and *service*, he writes: "There are different kinds of service (*diakonion*), but the same Lord" (1 Cor. 12:5 NIV).

In Paul's theology, the church is the Body of Christ. We are not all eyes, not all hands, not all ears—for the body needs the balance created by the full complement (i.e., variety, diversity) of its members. Every person who has been baptized into Christ has been set apart for the glory of God by the use of his or her natural gifts for service to Jesus, as well as through whatever additional Spirit-giftings may be granted.

This Pauline view of the church as a living organism in which every part contributes to health and function builds on the teachings of Jesus.

Over against both the Roman imperial power his Jewish contemporaries knew only too well and the rigid Jewish structures he was challenging, Jesus taught his followers not to behave as power brokers. "But it is not so among you; but whoever wishes to become great among you must be your servant (*diakonos*), and whoever wishes to be first among you must be slave (*doulos*) of all" (Mark 10:43–44 NIV).

Biblical scholar T. W. Manson captured the teaching of the New Testament on this point correctly by writing the following: "In the Kingdom of God service is not a stepping-stone to nobility: it is nobility, the only kind of nobility that is recognized."[1] Indeed, by reading the stories of Jesus and hearing him, we understand that he "came not to be served but to serve (*ouk elthen diakonethenai alla diakonesai*), and to give his life a ransom for many" (Mark 10:45).

He abandoned privilege to humble himself and wash the feet of his disciples on the very night one would have expected him to be self-absorbed and concerned about his impending fate. At the end of that episode—one in which William Willimon describes Jesus as "a servant of the servants at the Lord's Table"—Jesus gave a specific and clear command: "I have set you an example, that you also should do as I have done to you. Very truly, I tell you, servants (*doulos*) are not greater than their master" (John 13:15–16).

So why does a book that draws a contrast between a proffered pre-Christian Jesus and the Jesus of the contemporary church end with references to ministry and service? Why does its anticipated crescendo-summary focus on words such as "servant," "minister," and even the disquieting term "slave"? Quite simply, I believe the Jesus I know, love, recommend, and try to follow is the foot-washing servant of servants who cannot help but be appealing to all who know of him. On the other hand, the imperious, judgmental, and overbearing Jesus of Christendom is a dispiriting obstacle to those who are seeking God.

Something fateful and appalling happened in the fourth century. Whether from sincere-but-misguided faith or if-you-can't-beat-them-join-them manipulation, the Emperor Constantine embraced (and redefined!) Christianity. Contra Dan Brown and his farcical tales of Constantine's work at editing the Gospels and rewriting history, the emperor did something far worse. He took the Christian Gospels and their subversive language about serving, loving, and turning the other cheek and transformed them into state-sanctioned, state-enforced cultural norms of damnable religiosity. He turned the corporate expression of Jesus in the world into a tawdry religious corporation. The *over-against position* of Jesus and the persecuted organism called his church morphed into the *establishment-guarding* organization of the Middle Ages.

In post-Constantine Christianity, the power of transforming spirituality gave way to the dullness of status quo religion. Varieties of ministry by the diverse members of the Body of Christ gave way to a clergy-laity distinction in which the clergy "ministered" through sacerdotal performance and the laity observed passively. The church was no longer a dynamic organism but a place to go, a force with which to reckon, and a broker of power to be courted by the state. The new class called clergy ceased being objects of persecution and put on vestments to become persons of wealth, authority, and dignity. As a rule, they made it known to any community they entered that they had come not to serve but to be served. Jesus hadn't changed over the centuries, but the way he would henceforth be presented and viewed had now changed drastically.

I knew Jesus before he was a (post-Constantine, big-shot, uppity, privileged, hypercritical, disparaging, dismissive) *Christian*. It was back in the days that he was a servant to the servants and said we could find God in that same sort of simplicity. It was back when he stepped between rock-throwers and the guilty-as-sin people about to be stoned by them. It was in the times that he laughed, went to parties, held babies, touched blind people, ushered outcasts back into community, and otherwise showed humans the true nature of God. God is love. God is accepting and gentle. God is decent and holy, without being priggish about it. *And I liked him better then!*

Remember the student whose story I told early in this book? The African American who became a Jew after being placed in a foster home where security and love replaced the chaos and pain of a dutifully "Christian" home? It wasn't theology or argument that won him over and made him a convert. It was love, acceptance, and nurture over time that authenticated something to him and made it desirable. I'm not even sure his foster parents were trying to proselytize him. It just happened. They loved him enough that he began to be what they are.

The telling of his story in that day's class generated a writing project for him and the two dozen others in the room. They wrote and talked privately with me about their best and worst experiences of church. A predictable pattern emerged from the start. With not a single exception, the men and women who wrote of terrible things that made identification with the church difficult for them never raised an issue of biblical doctrine. Not one was having a problem with the church over Trinitarian theology, baptism, the millennium, or the nature of the bread and wine in the church's table event. Here were their problems: abandonment when her parents divorced, his abuse by a priest, constant bickering several had witnessed among church members, lack of compassion (or even presence) when her sister died, hypocrisy, "running my big sister off" when she got pregnant at sixteen, and so on.

The encouraging thing is that there were about as many stories that day from people who loved the church—always a local church, mind you, and never a denomination—on account of specific reasons they gave. Again, with not a single exception, the men and women who wrote of beautiful things that made a community of faith central to their lives and that had given them a vision of Jesus to embrace never cited an issue of doctrine or biblical theology. Okay. If you have challenged me in your mind to say that love, acceptance, and nurture are "doctrines" of the New Testament, you are spot-on correct. But that's not the way most of us use the terms. We split hairs over worship, hermeneutical method, soteriology, or pneumatology and call those "doctrinal matters"—while the world is going to hell for lack of love, acceptance, and caring.

I can't denounce theology and damn all the theologians. *For crying out loud, I* am *a theologian, and this book* is *an exercise in theology!* So don't get me wrong. The critical study of Scripture is central to faith. Faith, after all, comes by hearing, and what is heard comes through the word of Christ (see Rom. 10:17). But we need to do theology that is Christ-centered and other-centered, not institution-centered and other-dismissive.

Several years ago, Gordon MacDonald wrote a fascinating piece about the personal ministry of Jesus. He reflected on the possibility that "the way Jesus made his ministry happen might not be entirely acceptable among many orthodox and conservative organizations today."[2] I hadn't thought about that article for many years, until I ran across it the other day. Now that I have read it again, my guess is that it has influenced me more across the years than I had realized. It sums up many of the things this book attempts to say. MacDonald gives counsel and challenge at the end of his article that just might influence you to a healthier and higher view of Jesus for the sake of your faith in and service to him.

Here are MacDonald's six observations about Jesus' ministry style—a style the institutional church ignores to its detriment and that those who are beginning to prefer the pre-Christian Jesus just might appreciate.

1. Jesus spent the first thirty years of his life simply growing in stature and in favor with God and man. Immanuel (i.e., God among us) built bridges of understanding with family, neighbors, and fellow-Israelites before launching his rescue mission among them. He patiently built his credibility with people as his own personality, character, and faith were molded by the

Father. I have found that part of my challenge with many people these days is to build bridges and to win credibility among people who don't trust—no, just don't *like*—church people. They have been treated so badly by *some* people from *some* churches that they have a hard time believing *any* of us have a nonjudgmental, nonmercenary agenda.

2. The main focus of Jesus' ministry was building people. He would often move away from and shun big crowds in order to spend time on a few people that nobody thought would ever amount to much. Are we too obsessed with building big churches, big ministries, and big names for ourselves? Do we ever give the impression that those are our driving motives? God cares about persons, and persons have names and life situations that are complex. The Jesus I love loved people, so I want to learn to love them, too. And I believe God will bring the healing all of us need in Christ-centered communities of love and support for each other. Those communities are what the New Testament calls churches.

3. He refused to entangle himself in institutional activities. Yes, Jesus went to the temple and synagogue, but he spent most of his time teaching at parties, on boats, in fields, and walking along the road. In stark contrast to people then and now who measure success in terms of size, numbers, and dollars, he was content to seek and confer significance by being ordinary, unnoticed, and powerless. Your church doesn't need to battle for institutional and parachurch approval. You don't need validation by being the biggest, loudest, and pushiest bunch of people in town. And forget about building a base of alternative institutional clout in the face of people who don't get who you are trying to be. Christ's people serve and minister and give. The only authority we need to pursue is the kind Jesus had—the "moral authority" that comes of having integrity before the Lord.

4. Jesus was big on denouncing injustice and self-righteousness but spent precious little time debating theology. He vehemently censured those who tried to set themselves up as judges of others' spirituality, but he was not inclined to condemn those who were at least traveling in the same direction with him. That is the immediate and primary point of the episode told at Mark 9:38–41. People don't have to be "one of us"—a member of your denomination or someone who sees everything the way you see it—to be known by Christ and blessed by him.

5. Jesus always seemed more concerned about people's hearts than their heads. He was always compassionate with women who had been immoral and men who were corrupt. But he was angriest when dealing with religious leaders and power brokers. Nobody can love the weak, pursue the powerless, and treat disreputable people with kindness without being suspect in a religious culture. What a tragic irony! What a wicked truth!

6. The ultimate foundation for his whole ministry was his intimate relationship with the Heavenly Father. He drew strength from his Father's words. He continually withdrew from the crowds to spend time in prayer. And the Father constantly affirmed him by blessing what he did. For every hour of public teaching, there were many hours more spent in prayer, in small-group training, and in compassionate ministry to wounded people.

These significant hallmarks of Jesus' ministry style could still serve to guide those of us who confess him. They could be used in place of the institutional benchmarks that so often make church look more like a big corporation than a healthy family. If we submit to the simple kingdom reign of Jesus, then we can have the blessing of heaven by which to bless others. We can minister grace, healing, and power to broken souls. We can live even with whatever antagonism or contempt others feel compelled to fling in our direction. And we will pray for God to give us an opportunity to return good for evil—with a gentle, gracious spirit.

All the while, our task is to follow where he leads and to have the mind of Christ on the journey. To be filled with the Spirit. To be children of the

Father in Heaven. The practical outworking of these heavy theological burdens is the light and natural (to persons who have been born from above!) task of *living joyously before God's smiling face* (i.e., in holiness, set apart for God) and *extending that smile to others* (i.e., by compassion, loving our neighbors).

> Quit your worship charades. I can't stand your trivial religious games: monthly conferences, weekly Sabbaths, special meetings—meetings, meetings, meetings—I can't stand one more! Meetings for this, meetings for that. I hate them! You've worn me out! I'm sick of your religion, religion, religion, while you go right on sinning. When you put on your next prayer-performance, I'll be looking the other way. . . . Clean up your act. Sweep your lives clean of your evildoings so I don't have to look at them any longer. Say no to wrong. Learn to do good. Work for justice. Help the down-and-out. Stand up for the homeless. Go to bat for the defenseless. (Isa. 1:13–17 MSG)

> I hate all your show and pretense—the hypocrisy of your religious festivals and solemn assemblies. I will not accept your burnt offerings and grain offerings. I won't even notice all your choice peace offerings. Away with your noisy hymns of praise! I will not listen to the music of your harps. Instead, I want to see a mighty flood of justice, an endless river of righteous living. (Amos 5:21–24 NLT)

> Those who consider themselves religious and yet do not keep a tight rein on their tongues deceive themselves, and their religion is worthless. Religion that God our Father accepts as pure and faultless is this: to look after orphans and widows in their distress and to keep oneself from being polluted by the world. (James 1:26–27 NIV)

If that sounds either too idealistic or too impractical, perhaps it shows that what we have come to call Christianity has blurred our vision of Jesus. If that is the case, then we need to dig beneath the debris of religious rituals and conventions that have accumulated across the centuries to reclaim and live the vibrant gospel that once turned the world upside down—and could do so yet again.

NOTES

Introduction

1. Emo Philips, "The best God joke ever—and it's mine!" *The Guardian* (London), Sept. 29, 2005, www.guardian.co.uk/stage/2005/sep/29/comedy.religion.

2. For more on this documentary, see the official website: http://lordsaveusthemovie.com/. See also Dan Merchant, *Lord, Save Us from Your Followers* (Nashville: Thomas Nelson, 2008).

Chapter One

1. Stephen King, *On Writing: A Memoir of the Craft* (New York: Pocket Books, 2002), 52.

2. Samuel J. Stone, "The Church's One Foundation," 1866.

Chapter Two

1. *Chocolat*, directed by Lasse Hallström (Burbank: Buena Vista Home Entertainment, 2000), DVD.

2. Michael Frost and Alan Hirsch, *The Shaping of Things to Come: Innovation and Mission for the 21st-Century Church* (Peabody, MA: Hendrickson Publishers, 2003), 62.

3. In my opinion, the protest of Nietzsche's Madman that "God is dead," "We have killed him," and "Churches [are] the tombs and sepulchers of God" is understood correctly in terms of Bonhoeffer's position as explained in the text rather than the infamous God-is-dead language of Thomas J. J. Altizer in the 1960s. The critical section from Nietzsche may be found in *The Gay Science* (1882, 1887); translated by Walter Kaufmann in *The Portable Nietzsche* (New York: Viking Press, 1968), 95–96.

4. *Barcelona, Berlin, New York: 1928–1931*, ed. Clifford J. Green, trans. Douglas W. Stott, vol. 10, *Dietrich Bonhoeffer Works* (New York: Fortress Press, 2008), 354; quoted in Eric Metaxas, *Bonhoeffer: Pastor, Martyr, Prophet, Spy—A Righteous Gentile vs. the Third Reich* (Nashville: Thomas Nelson, 2010), 84. Metaxas traces the development of Bonhoeffer's thought in relation to "the shocking capitulation of the German church to Hitler in the 1930s" (p. xv) and in a way that parallels the thesis of this volume. It is his interpretation of the term "religionless Christianity" that is followed in the text.

5. Metaxas, *Bonhoeffer*, 467.

Chapter Three

1. Herod was not a Jew, and he applied his considerable skills as a builder to a temple-beautification project that he hoped would endear him to the Jewish people over whom he had persuaded the Romans to make him a vassal "king." The comment at John 2:20 that the temple had been under construction for forty-six years when Jesus challenged what went on in that place dates this initial Passover of John's Gospel at AD 27. As an interesting historical tidbit, it is ironic that the renovation of the larger site was finished only a few years before the Romans demolished the temple in AD 70. The so-called "Wailing Wall" (i.e., Western Wall) is all that remains of that structure.

There is also an episode in which Jesus cleanses the temple related in the Synoptic Gospels (see Matt. 21:12–13; Mark 11:15–17; Luke 19:45–46) that takes place during the fourth and final Passover of Jesus' life. Although there is considerable scholarly discussion on the topic, I do not believe the Synoptic writers and John are telling the same story—with either John or the other three writers mistaken about the timing. Jesus apparently "cleansed" the temple in AD 27 and caught the authorities completely off-guard with his anger and indignation; when he did the same thing three years later, they were watching him closely and prepared to take him on and deal with him.

2. Walter Brueggemann, *The Message of the Psalms* (Minneapolis: Augsburg Press, 1984), 49.

Chapter Five

1. John R. W. Stott, *The Cross of Christ* (Downers Grove, IL: InterVarsity Press, 1986), 255.

2. Fred B. Craddock, *Craddock Stories*, ed. Mike Graves and Richard F. Ward (St. Louis: Chalis Press, 2001), 156–157.

3. There are also several negative "one another" texts, such as: "Therefore let us stop passing judgment on one another" (Rom. 14:13 NIV); "If you keep on biting and devouring each other, watch out or you will be destroyed by each other" (Gal. 5:15); "Do not lie to each other, since you have taken off your old self with its practices" (Col. 3:9). The passages named in the chapter are positive in tone.

Chapter Six

1. Jaroslav Pelikan, interview, *U.S. News & World Report*, June 26, 1989.

2. Although it is not true that all suffering is the direct consequence of sin in the sufferer's life, this paralyzed man's appears to have been (John 5:14; see 9:1–12; Luke 13:1–8). He had suffered for thirty-eight years, and the attitude of some must have been that he was getting what he deserved. That wasn't the attitude of the compassionate Christ toward him.

Chapter Seven

1. John Eldredge, *Wild at Heart: Discovering the Secret of a Man's Soul* (Nashville: Thomas Nelson Publishers, 2001), 180–181.

2. Marnie Ferree graciously wrote and shared this testimony at my request. Information about her ministry may be found at http://BethesdaWorkshops.org. See Marnie Ferree, *No Stones: Women Redeemed from Sexual Addiction*, 2nd ed. (Downers Grove: InterVarsity Press, 2010).

Chapter Eight

1. Abraham Heschel, *Between God and Man: An Interpretation of Judaism* (New York: Fress Press Paperbacks, 1997), 161.

2. *Latreia* is as flexible as the English term "worship." It embraces a range of meanings that includes a Sunday morning church assembly to a more generic sense of devotion and service offered to the Lord.

3. Abraham Heschel, *I Asked for Wonder*, ed. Samuel H. Dresner (New York: Crossroad, 1983), 20.

4. Eugene Peterson, *Christ Plays in Ten Thousand Places* (Grand Rapids: Eerdmans, 2005), 113–114.

5. Rodney Clapp, *A Peculiar People* (Downers Grove, IL: InterVarsity Press, 1996), 95–96.

Chapter Nine

1. Charita Goshay, "Why is Jesus getting such bad P.R.?", *The Holland (MI) Sentinel*, April 11, 2010, A11.

2. Ibid.

3. The report *American Nones: The Profile of the No Religion Population* (based on the American Religious Identification Survey 2008) may be found online at www.american-religionsurvey-aris.org/reports/NONES_08.pdf.

4. Quoted in Michelle Boorstein, "15 Percent of Americans Have No Religion; Fewer Call Themselves Christians; Nondenominational Identification Increases," *Washington Post*, March 9, 2009, A04.

5. George Barna, *Revolution* (Wheaton, IL: Tyndale, 2005), 13–14.

6. Leonard Pitts Jr., "Religion is driving people away from God," *Houston Chronicle*, March 16, 2009, 5.

7. Charita Goshay, "Why is Jesus getting such bad P.R.?"

Chapter Ten

1. Tony Campolo, *The Kingdom of God Is a Party* (Nashville: Thomas Nelson, 1992).

2. Ibid.

3. Charles R. Taber, "In the Image of God: The Gospel and Human Rights," *International Bulletin of Missionary Research* (July 2002): 99.

4. N. T. Wright, *Simply Christian: Why Christianity Makes Sense* (San Francisco: HarperCollins, 2006), 140.

5. Taber, "In the Image of God," 102.

6. He explored this obligation later: "For though I am free with respect to all, I have made myself a slave to all, so that I might win more of them. To the Jews I became as a Jew, in order to win Jews. To those under the law I became as one under the law (though I myself am not under the law) so that I might win those under the law. To those outside the law I became as one outside the law (though I am not free from God's law but am under Christ's law) so that I might win those outside the law. To the weak I became weak, so that I might win the weak. I have become all things to all people, that I might by all means save some. I do it all for the sake of the gospel, so that I may share in its blessings." (1 Cor. 9:19–23)

7. Features of the discussion of modernity versus postmodernity in this chapter are framed by the discussion of six Christian leaders who were interviewed about the "possibilities and limits of postmodernism" for *Christianity Today* at www.christianitytoday.com/ct/2000/013/7.74.html.

Chapter Eleven

1. English translations variously render the term *huperetes* as "minister," "officer," "attendant," etc. The article on the Greek word in the *Theological Dictionary of the New Testament* points to the fact that a *huperetes* learns his task and receives his goal from a superior's direction. The word is a compound term that literally means "an under-rower" and may have been used originally to identify slaves who pulled the oars of a ship.

2. www.brunswickchurch.org/guests/ministers.php; see the original article: Harry Heintz, "Amateurize Your Church," *Leadership Journal* (Summer 1999).

3. There is certainly historical evidence that the so-called *monarchical episcopate* (i.e., a single bishop who supervised other church leaders) was beginning to emerge in some places in the second and third centuries. The fourth-century realignment of the church as an institutional entity with state protection and tutelage quickly created a more formal and widespread hierarchy of officers to administer its people, activities, and properties.

4. Walter L. Liefeld, *The NIV Application Commentary: 1 & 2 Timothy, Titus* (Grand Rapids, Mich.: Zondervan, 1999), 117. "It is noteworthy that here in 1 Timothy 3:1 Paul defines being an overseer in terms of function ('a noble task'), not of status or office. He is not encouraging people to seek status but responsibility. Whether this responsibility is *also* an 'office' depends partly on the meaning we assign to the word."

5. In the world of the New Testament, male "headship" in both home and church is presumed. There are female deacons (Rom. 16:1; see 1 Tim. 3:11), prophets (Acts 21:8–9; see 1 Cor 11:5), teachers (Acts 18:27), and the like in the original church. But there is no hint

of female elders. This seems to reflect the fact that the priesthood of all believers allowed males and females to function freely in areas of their giftedness. But the specific responsibility of oversight was reserved to males in family (Eph. 5:22–24) and church (1 Cor. 14:33b–35) settings. Whether these were temporary cultural conditions accommodated by the apostles (as with their non-assault on slavery) or matters of the divine will across time and cultures is a question being wrestled with by Christians from all our tribal groups.

Chapter Twelve

1. Rodney Clapp, *A Peculiar People: The Church as Culture in a Post-Christian Society* (Downers Grove, Ill.: InterVarsity Press, 1996), 165.

2. Ibid., 171.

3. Nicholas D. Kristof, "Who Can Mock This Church?" *New York Times,* May 2, 2010, online archives, www.nytimes.com/2010/05/02/opinion/02kristof.html.

4. "Letter to Diognetus," ed. and trans. Eugene R. Fairweather in *The Library of Christian Classics, Vol. 1: Early Christian Fathers* (Philadelphia: Westminster Press, 1953), 216–218.

Conclusion

1. T. W. Manson, *The Church's Ministry* (London: Hodder & Stoughton, 1948), p. 27.

2. Gordon MacDonald, "Strange Things, Strange People, Strange Places: The Unorthodox Ministry of Jesus," *Discipleship Journal* (Sept/Oct 1991): 32–34.

Discussion Guide

Introduction

How has the name of Jesus suffered devastating blows of credibility over time?

What bumper stickers really make you angry? Why?

If you could make your own bumper sticker for your faith, what would it be?

Chapter One
Pro-Jesus and Pro-Church

Is it possible to be pro-Jesus and pro-church at the same time? Explain your answer.

Stephen King wrote, "[W]hile I believe in God, I have no use for organized religion." How do you respond when a friend says this? How do others respond if you have said it?

How did Pharisees pigeon-hole people as sinners? Have you ever seen this happen in Christian contexts? If so, what was the effect?

How did Jesus enter the religious sub-culture and change the way sinners were viewed? Does the church have the responsibility to "imitate Jesus" in this? How might that happen?

Do you really think Jesus fits Christianity's institutional mold any better than he fit the one Judaism offered him?

Which denomination do you think Jesus Christ would join today? Or do you think he just might not choose to be part of any of our churches—mainline, evangelical, nondenominational, or otherwise?

Read James 1:27. Do you think James saw a distinction between what was passing as "religion" and authentic, God-affirming "spirituality" in his day? And this was written only about fifteen years after the Pentecost birthday of the church.

Chapter Two
The Church of Sanctified Religiosity

Frost and Hirsch, in their book, *The Shaping of Things to Come,* say Armanda's birthday party in the movie, *Chocolat,* "reminded us of Matthew's party for Jesus (Mark 2:15) where the outcasts, sinners, and tax collectors celebrated with the Messiah. Like Jesus, Vianne has collected the outcasts, the misfits, and created a veritable feast in their honor." If possible, watch this scene from the movie for yourself. The movie is available on DVD.

Have you ever been to a party like this where outcasts were invited and held in high honor? If so, describe the scene. What was its effect on you?

Agree or Disagree: *Church as it has been done for the past 1700 years has failed profoundly and needs to be abandoned.* Discuss.

Let me repeat that the gospel is both other than and greater than any cultural impediments to its ability to reach to, capture, and redeem people. It got through the layers of legalistic religion in Jerusalem in the first century. It penetrated the moral and philosophic bankruptcy of Greek thought in Athens, Corinth, and Rome. And it was the source of hope and salvation to thousands upon thousands in the medieval and modern periods of history that have followed.

But the fact remains that Christians of every generation and geographic placement, from every background and belief, with whatever cultural baggage or advantage – all of us should ask ourselves about God's will for us as we await Christ's return.

In light of the above reading, what does God want us to be doing in *our* time and place?

What are some obstacles to the gospel that we need to remove?

Do you think there are better ways to live and teach the gospel than we have used to date? If so, make some specific suggestions as to how it can be done.

Or, if we shift the question farther from ourselves and more to God himself, perhaps we should ask: What options is God opening to those who love him? What things is he trying to teach us?

What opportunities has God created for communicating the gospel to people in our time?

Refer to the chart on pages 45-46. Discuss the contrasts between the Institutional Church and Relational Church. Can you think of other contrasts that should be included?

Chapter Three
"If You Love God, Burn the Church!"

Do you think we have captured the essence of what Jesus died to make possible in what we now call Christendom? Explain your answer.

Do you think we have it figured out so well in any one of our denominations that its mission now is to sit in judgment on all the other "brands" of church?

Is it only Judaism that has degenerated over time into customs, practices, and outcomes far removed from God's original purpose? Has the same thing not happened in our own Christian history?

What do you think would happen if Jesus showed up in Rome, London, New York, or Los Angeles today?

Which church would he join? Or would his eyes flash with anger? Or would he be pleased with how attentive we are to one another and how well we take care of each other?

Would he be impressed by our passion for representing him faithfully to the world both in terms of compassion and holiness?

Isn't it possible that some of us are insisting on the right to perpetual infancy in our faith-lives? Explain your answer.

Why do we complain so bitterly when life disappoints us? Why is it "unfair" that we suffer?

Churches are bad about getting in the way of people who simply want to see Jesus. Do you think your church could be getting in the way of people seeing Jesus? Explain without being overly critical or judgmental.

Chapter Four
Religion as "Gamesmanship"

What do you think of Anne Rice's decision to "give up on Christianity"?

So what *does* her "quitting Christianity" statement mean?

Has she decided now that God doesn't exist after all? Jesus was a fraud? The Bible is a myth?

Read Mark 12:13-27. Discuss this text in light of the thesis of this chapter.

What did these confrontations between Jesus and the religious leaders accomplish?

What kind of faith do you have right now: Indoctrination faith? Conformity faith? Commitment faith?

Chapter Five
The Medium Really Is the Message

Read Matthew 12:46-50. Why is this text appropriate to this chapter?

Was Jesus being disrespectful to his family or perhaps making a point about the importance of family relationships vs. relationships formed by faith?

"Anyone who loves his father or mother more than me is not worthy of me," he added. "Anyone who loves his son or daughter more than me is not worthy of me" (10:37).

Does the notion that a local church should be *a relational community of sinners in process of recovering the human stature God originally intended for us to bear* scare you? Excite you? Confuse you?

Alcoholics Anonymous has an intervention strategy that is taken right from the Bible and its directions about dealing with broken relationships are found in Matthew 18:15ff. But Matthew 18 presumes that we are functioning relationally rather than institutionally. Are we?

In order to have far greater credibility with our not-yet-Christian neighbors, what kind of behavior should we model consistently? What spiritual disciplines in your life help you do so?

Chapter Six
But Today Is the Sabbath!

What is the difference between *tradition* and *traditionalism*?

Why is tradition valuable to individuals, families, and churches?

What is there about traditionalism that is so dangerous?

What kind of traditionalism does our generation of believers tend to preserve?

Discuss these important concepts covered in the chapter: Inclusion, Affirmation, and Relationship. Why are these so critical to Christian faith?

Chapter Seven
Caught Red-Handed!

Why does God keep on pursuing people society views as "losers"?

We should also ask ourselves the question, Why does God keep on lavishing his love on me?

Explain your concept of *grace* from a key biblical text on the theme.

Do you sense that God is trying to connect with your heart right now? Is there something he may be calling you to do?

Discuss the following concepts covered in the chapter: crimson thread, stained thread, golden thread. Why are these important?

Chapter Eight
Learning to Play Well on the Road

Discuss this common notion: "Church is sacred; other settings are not." Where did we get such notions of the nature of reality?

How does the notion of a sacred-secular division square with Paul's notion of how our bodies and spirits simultaneously engage in the life of God? "Therefore, I urge you, brothers, in view of God's mercy, to offer your bodies as living sacrifices, holy and pleasing to God—this is your spiritual act of worship" (Rom. 12:1).

Quoting Abraham Heschel: "Worship is a way of seeing the world in the light of God." Explain his statement in your own words. Do you agree or disagree?

What is worship? Where is worship? When do we worship?

Unpack this statement: *"All of life is service to God, and worship is how we stay focused on that mission."*

How have modern and postmodern churches *both* impoverished worship?

What are two basic truths of worship and how do these truths impact your own worship?

Chapter Nine
Jesus Could Use a Good PR Agent

Does God need to be "defended"? What do you think of the notion that Jesus needs a PR agent in our generation?

Have Christians been good public relations people for Jesus Christ over the centuries? Explain your answer with specifics.

Is there a trend toward secularism in America? Why or why not?

Discuss these four qualities of life in Christ. To what degree has your church or family developed these qualities?

Passionate for the integration of faith and life. This typically not only means disciplined reading and study of Scripture but hands-on involvement in serving, sharing their faith, and helping the poor.

Committed to biblical truth. They appreciate basic biblical doctrine but cannot be content to study theology without serious accountability in their spiritual lives, a conscientious pursuit of moral integrity, and the conviction that true faith exhibits itself in obedience to Christ.

Focused on the person of Christ. The highest priority of a revolutionary is conscious and joyous surrender to Jesus Christ; to be a "full-time servant of God" in what Luther would call the priesthood of all believers is their calling.

Transformed lives. Revolutionaries believe the imitation of Christ produces radical, outrageous devotion to God that shows itself in nothing less than a transformed life that experiences love, joy, and peace in the Holy Spirit.

Chapter Ten
Church as Defender of Human Dignity

What is the core of the church's message?

With the dual understandings that different cultures require different approaches with the gospel but that all cultures are intended eventually to give way to a single new identity in Christ, what does all this mean to our place in history?

Specifically, what does it mean about preaching the cross?

Why does this chapter suggest anti-modernity as a more descriptive term than postmodernity?

What is the church's relationship to the Kingdom of God?

Chapter Eleven
The Ministry of Amateurs

What would it take to "amateurize" ministry in your church?

Does leadership in your church lean toward an authoritarian model or an empowering model? What do you think accounts for that?

Consider the following:
There are no junior heads, princes, or secondary lords. There is Jesus; then there are the rest of us. Those among us who have leadership gifts are to exercise them for the sake of building consensus but never as "lording it over those entrusted to you, but being examples to the flock" (1 Pet. 5:3).

Can you take this idea of "not lording it over those entrusted to you" to work with you tomorrow morning? Can you believe that what you will be doing tomorrow is as important in God's scheme of redemption as what we are doing on a Sunday morning? What experience in life has shown you this is true?

What are you gifted to do? How are you using that giftedness to honor Christ at this juncture in your life?

Chapter Twelve
Turning Church Upside Down

When you hear the word *church*, what comes to mind? What do you visualize? What images dominate?

Explain what it might look like if churches were microcosms of the Kingdom of God that focus the great variety of personalities, gifts, and passions of people to the single task of honoring God in the world?

What if Christians in one group affirmed other groups of Christians for their gifts that benefit the larger body of Christ? What kind of Spirit would ultimately prevail between those groups? For example, one church may do more to serve the city, while another church may offer deeper and more biblically-guided preaching, and another more inspirational worship.

What if all of these Christian groups built one another up in love and then looked for ways to serve and honor the non-Christians around them?

How do we become a "priesthood of all believers"?

If the claim that the earliest church was "turning the world upside down" was true in its time (cf. Acts 17:6), it certainly is *not* true today. So perhaps it is the church that needs to be turned upside down—how can that begin to happen today where you are?

About the Author

Rubel Shelly serves as president of Rochester College in Rochester Hills, Michigan. He is the author or co-author of more than thirty books, including *The Jesus Proposal* (Leafwood, 2003), *The Jesus Community* (Leafwood, 2005), and *The Names of Jesus* (Howard Books, 1999). He ministered for twenty-seven years with the Woodmont Hills Family of God in Nashville, Tennessee. During that time, he has also taught at Lipscomb University, Vanderbilt University School of Medicine, and Tennessee State University. He holds a Ph.D. from Vanderbilt University. He and his wife, Myra, have three grown children who have given them nine wonderful grandchildren to love and spoil.